The population dynamics of Nepal

Judith Banister
and Shyam Thapa

Number 78 • December 19

PAPERS OF THE EAST-WEST POPULATION INSTITUTE

JUDITH BANISTER, formerly a postdoctoral Research Fellow at the East-West Population Institute, is now a Demographer in the Foreign Demographic Analysis Division of the U.S. Bureau of the Census. SHYAM THAPA is a doctoral candidate in the Department of Sociology and the Population Studies and Training Center at Brown University. The authors' names are listed in alphabetical order to indicate their equal contributions to this paper.

Library of Congress Cataloging in Publication Data

Banister, Judith.
    The population dynamics of Nepal.

    (Papers of the East-West Population Institute ;
no. 78)
    Bibliography: p.
    1. Nepal—Population. I. Thapa, Shyam, 1949-
II. Title. III. Series.
HB3636.9.A3B36   304.6'09549'6   81-19444
                                                AACR2

CONTENTS

TABLES, MAPS, AND FIGURES

Tables

ACKNOWLEDGMENTS

We were both at the East-West Population Institute when we prepared the first and final drafts of this paper. We are grateful to Dr. Lee-Jay Cho, who made this joint endeavor possible and provided support for our work, and to Dr. Robert D. Retherford for facilitating the completion of the paper.

Thanks are due to the Nepal Family Planning/Maternal and Child Health (FP/MCH) Project, especially to Dr. Badri R. Pande for permission to use the 1976 Nepal Fertility Survey data. We are also indebted to the World Fertility Survey headquarters in London, especially to Drs. Iqbal Allam, V.C. Chidambaram, and John G. Cleland, who supplied the data tapes and acted promptly on our requests at different stages of the analysis. We are grateful to the Nepal National Commission on Population, in particular to Dr. Bedh Prakash Upreti for cooperation and assistance throughout the project.

Many individuals contributed to the completion of this monograph. Drs. Linda Martin, John McQuiston, Dennis J. O'Donnell, Durga Ojha, Fred Reed, and Louise Williams, and the anonymous reviewers read an earlier draft and supplied us with many valuable comments and suggestions. Drs. Noreen Goldman, David E. Mutchler, James A. Palmore, Peter C. Smith, and Robert Worth also read portions of the draft and made many helpful comments. None are, however, responsible for the contents or possible remaining errors.

We are grateful to Ms. Sandra Ward for her skill and care in editing the paper, to Ms. Lois Bender for typesetting the manuscript, and to Messrs. Gregory Chu and Clyde Kanehiro for their cartographic work. Last but not least, we greatly appreciate the assistance and consultation for computer programming of Mss. Ruby Bussen, Gayle Uechi, and Victoria Ho, and the typing assistance of Mss. Kathleen Lau and Carol Walker.

To all these persons and others who have contributed to the completion of this monograph, including the Office of Population, U.S. Agency for International Development, which supported our research and the publication of this monograph under contract no. AID/DS/PE-C-0002, we express our deep appreciation.

ABSTRACT   *Drawing upon censuses, survey reports, and other data sources including information from the 1976 Nepal Fertility Survey, this paper analyzes the demographic situation of Nepal within the broader context of recent economic, agricultural, and environmental changes. Over the period examined, from the early 1950s to the late 1970s, fertility has remained high. Mortality, though still high, has begun a gradual decline, and a trend toward lower infant mortality is evident. A trend toward later marriage is also underway, although it has not been sufficient to depress fertility. Nepal has had a national family planning program for over a decade, but knowledge and use of modern contraceptive methods overall are still at a very low level. Despite the government's efforts to provide family planning services throughout the country, inaccessibility of many rural villages remains an obstacle.*

   Nepal's isolation and mountainous topography have impeded other forms of modernization as well. The country's predominantly agricultural economy has barely kept up with population increase in recent years. Per hectare agricultural yields have actually declined, and increases in total agricultural production have come almost exclusively from the expansion of tilled acreage. The combination of rapid population growth, declining agricultural productivity, and reliance on wood as a fuel has resulted in deforestation and consequent soil erosion, floods, and landslides.

   One response to the dilemma of increasing population pressure, declining agricultural productivity, and deterioration of the environment has been accelerated population redistribution, mainly from the hills and mountains to the terai (lowland plains), where malaria was brought under control during the 1950s. The majority of migrants are male, attracted to the prospect of acquiring terai land. Because the country has not yet experienced much urbanization, rural-to-rural migration is the predominant redistribution process, although international migration between Nepal and neighboring countries, in particular India, continues to be substantial.

   Because of declining mortality and sustained high fertility, Nepal is likely to experience continued rapid population growth in the immediate future. The demographic momentum inherent in the young age structure of the population will result in a population of over 20 million by the end of this century. For a small mountainous country with

*already high population density on the arable land and a modest
known resource base, such growth will pose major economic, social,
and ecological problems.*

This monograph explores the population dynamics of Nepal, a developing country that in some ways is typical of many other developing countries and in other ways is unique. We present an assessment of the past and current population situation of the country, and discuss likely future population changes. Because rapid population growth has so powerful an effect on the society, the economy, and the environment, our demographic analysis naturally spills over into a discussion of these other aspects of Nepalese life. This monograph is written for a broad audience—for demographers, development experts, persons specializing in the study of Nepal, and also anyone interested in an overview of Nepal's current population situation and future population prospects.

Nepal is a small, landlocked Asian country (Map 1). Its unusual terrain presents special, perhaps even unique, problems of socioeconomic development and environmental preservation. East to west, Nepal is long and narrow. North to south, within a distance of about 160 air kilometers (100 miles), the terrain drops in altitude from Himalayan peaks averaging over 6,000 meters (20,000 feet) high, to nearly sea level at its southern border. This steep north-to-south drop gives Nepal an enormous hydropower potential but also contributes to soil erosion. Ecologically speaking, Nepal can be broadly categorized into three terrains: (1) the northern high altitude belt referred to as the mountains; (2) the middle belt called the hills, which is historically the most populated terrain; and (3) the southernmost portion of low-lying plains known as the "terai." Between the hills and the terai is the "inner terai."[1] The steep gorges, cut between high ridges, make transportation and communication in an east-west direction difficult or impossible except at the lowest altitudes. Major rivers cut the country into river valleys largely isolated from one another. Nepal's topography alone makes formidable the task of creating a viable national economy.

Although east-west transportation and communication at the higher altitudes are difficult, people move relatively easily in the north-south

---

1   For an overview of the geography of Nepal, see Karan with Jenkins (1960) and
    Hagen (1961).

MAP 1 The location of Nepal

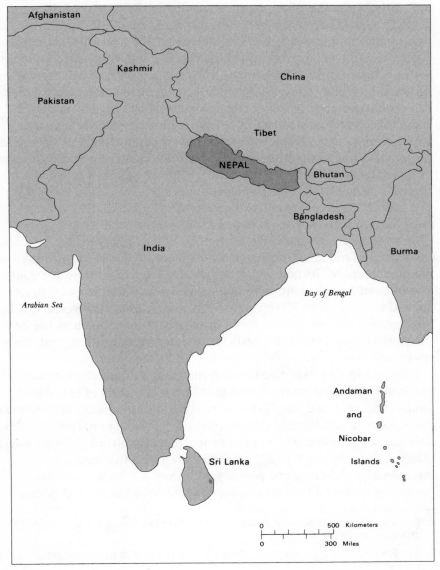

direction, through mountain passes and on trails and rivers in the river valleys. Part of the government's economic development strategy since the early 1970s, therefore, has been to divide the country into four development regions from west to east, with boundaries determined in part by natural mountain barriers.[2] Three of the development regions encompass one major river and its tributaries, and the fourth region is defined more on the basis of proximity to the politically dominant Kathmandu Valley (Map 2). Each development region has the Himalayan mountain range in the north, a portion of the terai in the south, and a hill section in between. The four regions vary in climate and population density. The Far Western Development Region has an arid climate and low population density. Rainfall increases toward the east. The Central and Eastern Development Regions have a wet monsoon climate and relatively high population density.

In part because of its unusual geography, Nepal has had a history quite different from that of most of the world's other developing countries. Nepal has never been colonized.[3] For many centuries it has successfully fended off threatened incursions by Tibet and China from the north, and by Britain and other potential invaders from the south. The price of Nepal's hard-won independence was that the country remained isolated from Western modernization until after World War II, thus missing possible benefits of European influence, such as the beginnings of industrialization, efficient transport, education, and modern health care.

From 1846 to 1951, Nepal was technically a monarchy but was autocratically ruled by the hereditary Prime Ministers of the Rana family. On one hand, the Ranas were successful in maintaining Nepal's independence and legitimizing its status as a sovereign nation in international law and practice. On the other, recent political analysts assert that the Rana family resisted all winds of change that might have threatened their status and power within Nepal.[4] Their pattern of vigorous defense of the status quo, coupled with intentional isolation

---

2   For a detailed discussion of regional development in Nepal, see Gurung (1969) and Okada (1970).

3   See Rose (1971) for a history of Nepal's long struggle to prevent annexation by foreign powers.

4   On the subject of legitimization of Nepal's sovereignty, see Rose (1971:55 ff.). For information on political, economic, and social conditions in Nepal during the Rana regime, see Kumar (1967:135 ff.).

MAP 2 The terrains and development regions of Nepal

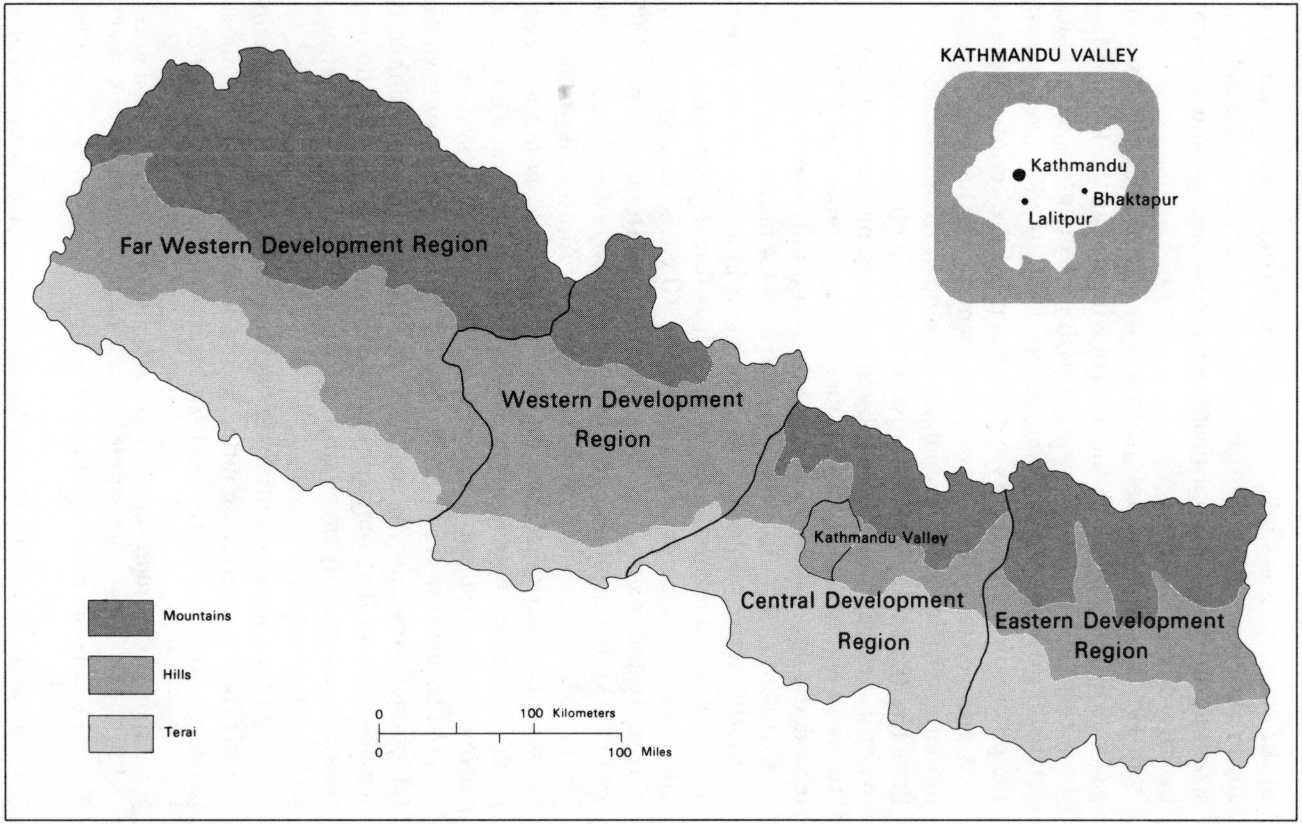

KATHMANDU VALLEY

Kathmandu
Bhaktapur
Lalitpur

Far Western Development Region

Western Development Region

Central Development Region

Eastern Development Region

Kathmandu Valley

Mountains

Hills

Terai

100 Kilometers

100 Miles

of the country, was similar to that of the Tokugawa Shogunate in Japan. Assessments by scholars focusing on the Rana period emphasize that its legacy was political, social, educational, and economic backwardness.[5]

In 1951 the Rana dictatorship was overthrown by a mass political party with the support of the *de jure* King under the Rana rule. For a short period, Nepal experimented with parliamentary democracy characterized by a multi-party system.[6] In 1960, the King reestablished the power of the monarchy, which has ruled the country since then.

A primary task of the government since 1951 has been to try to modernize the country. Nepal has been open to outside contact for a little less than three decades now. It has been changing dramatically over this period. Nevertheless, by almost any measure, the country is still at an early stage of development. For example, the 1971 census recorded a population 96 percent rural and only 4 percent urban (Nepal, CBS, 1977:36). As of that date, 94.4 percent of the economically active population were in the primary sector consisting of agriculture and related industries, such as forestry (Nepal, CBS, 1977: 206). Ninety-six percent of the females 10 years old and over, and 75 percent of the males aged 10 and over were illiterate (Nepal, CBS, 1977:203). Per capita income is still very low, estimated at about US $120 in 1978 (World Bank, 1980:110). Almost all production and consumption are concentrated in the subsistence, nonmonetized part of the economy. Few roads are suitable for vehicles and almost all movement and transport are on foot. The telephone system is restricted to the few urban centers; the rest of the country is without telephones. Government centers around the country are linked by a wireless system that functions poorly or not at all during the monsoon season, leaving many areas cut off from outside communication for part of the year.[7]

In spite of Nepal's continuing backwardness, it has not remained cut off from modernizing influences. The international system is more pervasive now than in the past, and can no longer be ignored or fended

---

5 Information regarding state revenue, agricultural production, food prices, industry, trade, and education during the Rana period is presented in Kumar (1967).

6 For a detailed account of this period see Joshi and Rose (1966) and Chauhan (1971: ch. 5).

7 For statistics on the number of kilometers of roads and the number of telephone lines, wireless stations, and airports, see Shreshtha and Jain (1978:56–57).

off. Since 1952, Nepal's government has opened up the country to international contact. Ideas and people now flow more readily into and out of Nepal, so that the central government and the elite are more aware of events and experiences elsewhere.

Another force irrevocably changing Nepal is rapid population growth. Malaria control in the terai and continuing public health work in major areas of the country since 1951 have considerably reduced mortality, while fertility has stayed at traditional levels, or even risen. The difference between fertility and mortality has produced an increasing rate of natural population growth, which in turn has set in motion other forces. There has been more and more crowding on the arable land, much internal migration to newly available land in the terai, intense competition for dwindling resources such as arable land and firewood, and more contact between previously isolated groups, with resulting tensions. The political system is facing pressures to fill many more roles and become more effective than in the past.

Nepal's rapid population growth thus gives urgency to the search for solutions to the country's socioeconomic problems. Yet its topography, history, and current situation are different enough from those of other countries to dictate caution. Models of development suitable for other developing countries may not be suitable for Nepal.

SOURCES OF INFORMATION ON NEPAL'S POPULATION

Data sources for analyses of the general levels and trends of mortality, fertility, and migration, as well as for other demographic measures of Nepal, are rather limited. As is typical of less developed countries, most of the available data on the population of Nepal are subject to misreporting and underreporting. Therefore, inferences based on such data warrant careful evaluation. Our purpose here is to discuss briefly some of the major sources.

Vital registration system

Until recently Nepal had no vital registration system. Now the government has begun recording vital events, but it will be some time before coverage is complete enough to permit national estimates of vital rates. The government expects that the vital registration system will be in operation throughout the country by the end of 1987.

Virtually all births occur in the home and still are not officially registered. Deaths usually occur outside hospitals, and also remain unregistered. A law passed in 1962 provides for legal registration of marriage and divorce, but such registration is not mandatory for all marriages and divorces. Therefore, most of these vital events still go unregistered.

Censuses

Because the vital registration system is in the early stages of implementation, demographic estimates for Nepal must be based on censuses and surveys. Before 1951, the only demographic information available came from population counts taken in 1911, 1920, 1930, and 1941.[8] The only surviving results of these counts are the total population enumerated each time, with no detail on age, sex, or other characteristics. The four counts were conducted by landlord agents who were also tax collectors, so that enumeration was not their primary task and might not have been done very conscientiously. Whole households might have had reason to avoid being counted if they could, to prevent any tax burden. These early population counts were probably less complete than Nepal's recent censuses.

The 1952/54 census was Nepal's first attempt at a modern census with internationally accepted definitions.[9] This census was taken under very difficult circumstances. The Rana oligarchy had just been overthrown and a new government system was being set up. Many of the people were probably suspicious of the census questions, most of which they had never been asked before. That the enumerators were mostly local tax collectors did not help to allay the public's fears. All the blank census forms had to be carried by foot on trails from Kathmandu. It took weeks or even months of walking for some census supervisors to reach their enumeration areas. After the census was taken, the supervisors accompanied the completed census forms back to Kathmandu by the same tortuous route. Then they spent two years tabulating 8.4 million individual data slips by hand, without office equipment of any kind.

There are problems of data quality with the 1952/54 census, as is to

---

8   Several sources describe what little is known about the first four population counts of this century, including the evidence for suspecting the quality of some of the counts more than others. See Nepal, CBS (1977:22); Krotki and Thakur (1971:89–91); and Nepal, Department of Statistics (1958:vi–viii).

9   For a discussion of how this census was carried out, see Nepal, Department of Statistics (1958:i–ii, vi–viii).

be expected from any country's first modern census. One of the more serious problems is that, because of civil disturbances, half of the country was counted in May 1952 whereas the other half was not enumerated until May 1954. Analysts have, in general, lumped the data from both parts of the census together as if the whole country had been enumerated simultaneously, a procedure that introduces new errors in addition to those present in the original data.

One careful analysis by Krotki and Thakur (1971) of the reported age-sex structures of the 1952/54 and the 1961 censuses explored sex ratios by age and census survival ratios by age, and compared the reported age-sex structures with a model stable age-sex distribution.[10] The authors concluded that there was strong evidence of serious undercounting of children under age 5, underenumeration of females aged 10—24, and underenumeration of males in the 15—24 age group in the 1952/54 census. Taken together, these age- and sex-selective undercounts suggest a minimum undercount of about 5 percent of the total population. The undercount may have been greater because whole households or whole villages could easily have been missed.

The 1961 census was probably an improvement over the 1952/54 one, although it had its own problems. It was taken during a time of political confusion just after the King had reestablished monarchial power in 1960. The 1961 census was a two-stage *de jure* count.[11] Census supervisors first went to each village in their jurisdiction and made a list of households including the total number of people in each household by sex as of May 1961. Some of these data were probably taken from village records. Then the enumerators, using the household list as a guide, carried out the complete household enumeration in June 1961. This census was also hand-tabulated, and the process took four and one-half years. An analysis by Krotki and Thakur (1971) of 1961 census data found a pattern of undercounting similar to that in the 1952/54 census: both sexes undercounted at ages 0—4, females undercounted at ages 10—19, and males undercounted at ages 15—24. Krotki and Thakur estimated a net underenumeration of 4.6 percent for the 1961 census.

The 1971 census was also a two-stage process, in which a preliminary

---

10 The demographic terms mentioned here and elsewhere in this monograph are defined in the glossary.

11 For a description of 1961 census procedures see Nepal, CBS (1977:11—12).

household count provided the frame for the subsequent enumeration.[12] This time the census schedule was pretested in two village *panchayats* (political units, each corresponding to a group of villages or a town) and one urban area. The enumerators were members of the local political leadership, often the village clerk, or school teachers. This was the first census precoded by the enumerators and processed by computer. Processing took one and one-half years.

For the June-July 1981 census, the government increased the census budget from $10 million, allocated for the 1971 census, to about $25 million.[13] Part of this cost increase reflects inflation, and part is due to an important shift in the method of paying enumerators. In all previous censuses, enumerators were paid according to the number of persons counted. This system rewarded speed at the expense of accuracy, making it expedient for enumerators to skip out-of-the-way households and to complete the forms from village records. Under the new method, enumerators are given a salary and additional allowances based on the number of miles covered and the means of conveyance.

Preparatory work for the 1981 census included more careful mapping of the households and villages in the country, which should facilitate more complete coverage of the population. One problem with all censuses so far, and the 1981 census as well, is that Nepal's internal political boundaries have changed between every two censuses. For example, there were nearly 4,000 panchayats at the time of the 1971 census; now boundaries have been rearranged and there are only about 2,900 panchayats for the 1981 census. Census mapping and enumeration are done according to the panchayat boundaries. Therefore, the tracing of intercensal population changes by means of collected census data will continue to be an arduous or impossible task for most localities. Urban and district boundaries have also changed from census to census, making it difficult to describe trends on municipal or district levels.

Demographic surveys

The other primary source of demographic information in Nepal is surveys. The quality of the surveys taken so far has varied enormously. One of the earliest surveys relevant to demographic analysis was the

---

12 Details on the conduct of the 1971 census are from Nepal, CBS (1977:6—11).

13 These details on the 1981 census are from Mr. Radha Krishna Gharty Chhetry of the Central Bureau of Statistics (personal communication).

Nepal Health Survey of 1965–66 (Worth and Shah, 1969). In that survey, the village was the sampling unit, and 24 villages throughout Nepal were randomly selected for in-depth interviewing. The random selection was taken from a map grid, with the mountains, hills, and terai represented in the sample in proportion to the total number of villages in each ecological zone. Unfortunately, the survey team ran out of resources and time before completing its work and had to skip six of the 24 villages, thus making it unlikely that the final sample of villages surveyed was fully representative of the total population of Nepal.

In every village covered by the survey, a public health team first described the general conditions of sanitation, food storage, water quality, housing, refuse disposal, pests, nutrition, education, and medical care. Then, a census was taken in every household of the village, household members were given medical tests to determine disease prevalence, and all women who had ever married were interviewed about their marriages, fertility, mortality of infants, and family planning attitudes. The collected fertility and child mortality data from the Nepal Health Survey appear to be of better quality than any Nepal census as of that period, with less undercounting of young children, and more complete reporting of children ever born, children surviving, and infant mortality.

The authors of the Nepal Health Survey (NHS) report, when discussing why certain NHS results were so much better than the corresponding 1961 census results, noted that "the 1961 census was done through a predominantly male line of communication, while our survey census was made house-to-house, with women talking to women" (Worth and Shah, 1969:28). All of the censuses so far have used male interviewers who usually questioned male heads of household or male village heads. This male-to-male pattern of enumeration may have been partly responsible for producing significant census undercounts of young children and underreporting of the fertility and child mortality experiences of households. Survey experience in Nepal over the years has shown that these particular reporting problems can be alleviated by questioning women in the households. In addition, in-depth survey interviews tend to elicit more complete fertility and mortality responses than do very short interviews characteristic of a census.

For a decade after the Nepal Health Survey, no surveys directly relevant to national demographic estimation, public health, or family planning were conducted in Nepal. Then during the first half of 1975, a Nutrition Status Survey was carried out by the United States Center for Disease Control in cooperation with the U.S. Agency for International Development and the Government of Nepal, to ascertain the nutritional status of rural Nepalese children. Two hundred and twenty-one sample sites (villages) were chosen by the fixed interval method of population proportionate sampling (United States, Center for Disease Control, et al., 1975:9–12, 55–62). Thirty children of ages six months to six years were selected from about ten randomly chosen households in each sample site, for a total surveyed population of 6,566 children throughout rural Nepal. Data from the 1975 Nepal Nutrition Status Survey appear to be representative of the rural population of Nepal.

The survey had a narrow purpose, which was to determine whether children showed certain physical signs of nutritional deficiency, in particular as evidenced by their height and weight in relation to their age. Children who were very short for their reported ages were defined as "stunted" by long-term nutritional inadequacy, whereas children with very low weight in relation to their height were defined as "wasted" by recent acute nutritional deficiency. The conclusions of this survey depend crucially on the anthropometric theory behind these definitions. One problem with the definition of stunting is that children of any age naturally exhibit great variation in height, based on their genetic makeup alone. Short children have not necessarily been nutritionally deprived, but the crude anthropometric definition of stunting used in this survey would classify naturally short children as stunted, even if they had had adequate nutrition all their lives. The definition of stunting in the case of Nepal is also problematic because of age misreporting. For example, there tends to be heaping on the reported age of five years (see section on age reporting and age structure), and many of the children reported as five years old were actually younger. The Nepal Nutrition Status Survey might call a four-year-old child stunted because the child was short for a five-year-old and the child's age was reported as five years. The definition of wasting used in the survey is probably more valid than the definition of stunting, because no age reporting was incorporated into the definition of wasting as low weight for height. When interpreting the results of the Nepal Nutrition Status Survey, one should bear in mind the possible weaknesses of these anthropometric definitions.

A second survey relevant to population analysis began in 1975 and was conducted in four successive rounds through 1978. This was a small family planning KAP survey (i.e., of knowledge, attitudes, and practices concerning family planning) in two hill districts and two terai districts, organized by the Nepal Family Planning/Maternal and Child Health Project (Tuladhar and Stoeckel, 1975). After the first round of the survey, two more districts were added. The purposes of this KAP Baseline Survey were to document the attitudes toward family planning in Nepal, to determine how much contraceptive use there was already, to identify which women might be most receptive to family planning motivational work, to document differences and similarities between hill and terai women, and to provide a data base with which to compare future progress in family planning acceptance in Nepal. The survey was useful for most of its intended purposes, but the districts chosen were not representative of the whole country. Therefore it is not feasible to estimate Nepal's national vital rates from these survey data.

A longitudinal survey known as the Demographic Sample Survey of Nepal (DSS) was carried out during the years 1974—78 by the Central Bureau of Statistics in cooperation with the United Nations (Bourini, 1976 and 1977; Nepal, CBS, 1978). The purpose of the survey was to fill the gap in demographic statistics and provide accurate estimates of fertility, mortality, and migration for Nepal. Unfortunately, the DSS had several serious problems that resulted in questionable data quality. The sample was not representative of the country as a whole, vastly overrepresenting hill areas, seriously underrepresenting the terai, and misrepresenting the mountains by the deliberate choice of two mountain areas uncharacteristically accessible by airplane (Bourini, 1976: 4—6, and 1977: preface; Nepal, CBS, 1977:28). The distortion of the sample makes it risky to extrapolate from the 0.6 percent of Nepal's population interviewed to the entire population of Nepal.

The basic idea behind this longitudinal survey was a good one, however. Each sample household was enumerated every six months, with births and deaths and migrations recorded for the last six-month period. Such a survey methodology should minimize problems of recall, because events being reported are so recent. But the conduct of the survey did not live up to its potential. Only male interviewers were hired. They interviewed male heads of household or male village heads to obtain the data. The DSS was a low-budget operation. Enumerators were

instructed to cover 30—40 households per day, thus placing greater
emphasis on speed than on other considerations (Bourini, 1976:54).
In addition, all the usual problems with census results in Nepal were
duplicated in this survey. Infants and young children were under-
enumerated; births were underreported; infant and child deaths were
underreported; adult deaths were underreported. Therefore fertility
and mortality estimates were all clearly low and had to be inflated by
some inflation factor.

The inflation factors for each year of the survey were derived from
a postenumeration matching check. Ten percent of the enumerated
households were interviewed. An attempt was made to match the
births and deaths reported in the survey and in the control check. Any
vital events not matched were assumed to be real events missed by
either the survey or the control check. The survey results were then
inflated by the addition of unmatched vital events from the control
check. There were two major obvious problems with this procedure.
First, perfect matching in surveys is notoriously difficult to do. It is
likely that many of the unmatched events were really the same births
or deaths being reported both in the survey and in the control check;
but because of slight differences in spelling of a person's name or in a
date of birth or death, the independently reported events were not
properly matched. Second, the control sample was too small. The
somewhat arbitrary fertility and mortality inflation factors were derived from fewer than 300 births and fewer than 125 deaths. Random
error or random fluctuations could play a large role owing to the
small sample. Therefore, fertility and mortality estimates from the
DSS should be viewed with caution.

The most recent nationwide demographic survey taken in Nepal,
and perhaps the best ever taken, was the Nepal Fertility Survey of
1976 (NFS). This survey was part of the World Fertility Survey, an
international effort to collect comparable data using the same basic
questionnaire for many countries. The work in Nepal was planned and
carried out by the Family Planning/Maternal and Child Health
(FP/MCH) Project, aided by an advisory group from the University of
California at Berkeley, and by the International Statistical Institute in
London. The sample was designed as a self-weighting probability sample so that the mountains, hills, and terai would be represented in the
sample in proportion to their population sizes (Nepal, FP/MCH Project, 1977). The first stage of rural sample selection was to choose 33

of Nepal's 75 districts with probability proportional to the size of each district's 1971 census population. Then two rural panchayats were systematically drawn from each of the 33 chosen districts, again with probability proportional to the census population. Finally, a random sample of one or two wards (political units of about 20 to 100 households each) was chosen from each rural panchayat; 96 rural wards were selected from throughout the country. The urban sample, representing only 4 percent of Nepal's population, was drawn separately through a similar procedure. Altogether, 5,976 households were identified in the selected sample areas. Fertility and mortality estimates derived from the NFS can safely be assumed to be representative of all Nepal, unless serious response errors are detected, though subject to the limitations of sampling error inherent in all sample surveys.

The purpose of the 1976 NFS was to estimate the levels and trends of fertility and child mortality, as well as the prevalence of contraceptive use in the country. An interviewer went to each of the selected households and first took a census of all household members. Then the interviewer identified all ever married women of reproductive age (15–49) in the household, and proceeded to take a complete pregnancy history of each such eligible woman. The total number of women interviewed was 5,940. The individual questionnaire for eligible women had been pretested and adjusted with the purpose of eliciting cooperation and accurate responses concerning respondents' ages, marital histories, fecundity, births, infant and child deaths, children still living, attitudes toward family planning, etc. In addition, the questionnaire had built-in requirements for detecting and correcting internal inconsistencies in the data being reported, and for probing for complete reporting of births and deaths. The enumerators were experienced, intensively trained, and thoroughly supervised in the field. The result was rather complete reporting of fertility and child mortality for the 15 years prior to the survey, indicating that it requires no major upward adjustment. An evaluation of the NFS data has been carried out by Goldman et al. (1979). They point out that there were errors in the reporting of age, duration of marriage, and duration of breastfeeding, and they question the accuracy of the fertility data for earlier decades— based on an assumption of constant fertility during the 35 years prior to 1976. But they agree that the NFS achieved more complete coverage of Nepalese infant and child mortality than any other recent survey, and that the respondents gave essentially complete reports of their fertility in the years immediately prior to the survey.

Why was the 1976 NFS relatively successful in providing fertility and infant mortality estimates for Nepal, compared with all previous censuses and most surveys with their serious underreporting of fertility and mortality? First, the sample design was a good one. Second, the NFS was adequately funded, and interviewers were provided with helicopter transport to remote areas, which made the whole process much more efficient than it would have been if trekking over trails had been required. Third, it was the women of the household who answered the questionnaires. Fourth, the survey design allowed ample time for the interviewer to establish rapport with the respondent and to draw out her relevant knowledge and attitudes. Finally, the whole survey was skillfully designed, pretested, carried out, coded, edited, and analyzed by an international team of demographers from Nepal and other countries.

The NFS is the best source yet available for the estimation of recent fertility and infant and child mortality. Censuses and other surveys can be used to fill some of the gaps in demographic knowledge of Nepal. Besides the NFS, the Nepal Health Survey and KAP Baseline Survey provide valuable information on unwanted fertility, ideal family size, contraceptive use, availability of family planning services, and attitudes toward birth control. The censuses provide data on education, literacy, occupation, the rural-urban distribution of the population, and other indicators of economic and social development that help describe Nepal's progress or lack of it. All this information is useful for analyzing the demographic situation in Nepal.

AGE REPORTING AND AGE STRUCTURE

Nepal has had poor age reporting in all censuses and surveys, an experience common to most South Asian and African countries, though the exact patterns of age misreporting differ. It is not the fault of the census or survey procedures, but rather is due to the lack of importance attached to one's exact date of birth or exact current age. When an interviewer asks respondents when they were born or how old they are, or the date of their child's birth or the age at which someone has died, the answer is usually approximate. In some instances, the respondent is unable or unwilling to give an answer. In the latter situation, the interviewer has to supply an educated guess, based on other criteria such as the respondent's life experiences in reference to particular historical or social events or whether the respondent is married and how many children the respondent has. Figure 1 shows the ages of the surveyed population as reported from the Nepal Fertility Survey household interviews in 1976. If age reporting were accurate, we would expect to find a slightly smaller percentage of the total population in each successive single year of age, with possible modifications due to age-selective international migration flows, significant changes in fertility, or sharp mortality fluctuations. Instead, we see, for example, that four times as many people were reported to be age 40 as 41. This anomaly is due to severe "heaping" on age 40 and avoidance of nearby ages ending in digits like 9 and 1.

This kind of age misreporting can have serious consequences for demographic analysis. If age reporting were perfect, successive Nepal censuses could be used to give fairly accurate estimates of levels and trends in fertility and mortality that gave rise to that age structure. Moreover, with good reporting of the ages of mothers and their children, a fertility history could be reconstructed for the years prior to the survey, which would accurately portray the level of fertility for each age group of women for each year. But severe age misreporting has distorted the estimation of fertility and mortality based on the reported age distribution. For example, if a woman reported in 1976 that she was 40 years old and had borne a daughter five years earlier who was now five years old, this should mean that in about 1971 the woman had a birth at the age of 35. But if she was actually 37 years old at the time of the survey, not 40 as reported, and her daughter was actually six years old, then the birth happened in about 1970 when the woman was 31 years old. The result of such age misreporting is that the birth is allocated to the wrong year and to the wrong age of the mother, thus distorting the trends in fertility over time and the age-specific fertility rates at any one time.

Though age heaping was pronounced in the 1976 Nepal Fertility Survey, it was even worse in Nepal's 1971 census. Table 1 presents an index of age heaping that measures the extent of preference for some terminal digits and avoidance of others. Respondents in Nepal showed a strong preference for numbers ending in 0 and 5, and a tendency to avoid most other digits.

To smooth out most distortions caused by age misreporting, single-year data can be cumulated into five-year age groups. Figure 2 shows the reported age data for males and females by five-year age groups, unadjusted for age misreporting. The reported age distributions for

FIGURE 1 Single-year age distribution of the total population: Nepal, 1976 NFS

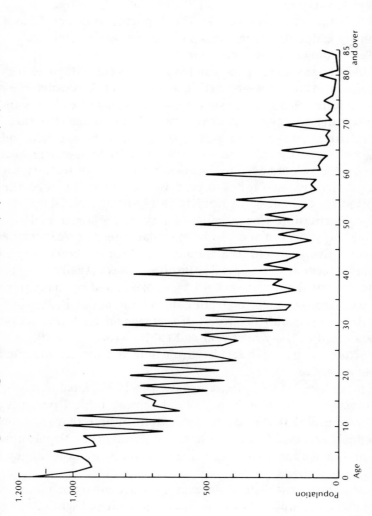

NOTE: The age distributions shown here are based on the NFS household data tape. There is a slight discrepancy between these data and the data reported in the NFS (Nepal, FP/MCH Project, 1977:236—37), because some cases were missing from the early data tape used for that volume. Throughout our analysis, the household data refer to the complete data tape.

TABLE 1 Index of age preference for Nepal by sex: 1971 census and 1976 NFS Household Survey

| | Deviation from 10.0% (signs disregarded) | | | | | |
| | 1971 | | | 1976 | | |
Terminal digits	Male	Female	Both sexes	Male	Female	Both sexes
0	10.7	13.8	12.3	9.5	8.7	9.1
1	3.7	4.0	3.9	3.8	2.9	3.3
2	1.2	0.7	0.9	2.4	1.5	1.9
3	4.8	5.0	4.9	3.4	3.0	3.2
4	3.8	3.7	3.7	2.8	2.5	2.7
5	10.2	9.6	9.9	7.4	5.8	6.6
6	1.9	2.7	2.3	1.4	1.0	1.2
7	4.2	4.6	4.4	3.5	3.6	3.5
8	1.3	1.2	1.3	0.4	0.4	0.4
9	5.1	5.3	5.2	3.9	3.3	3.6
Summary index of age preference	23.5	25.3	24.4	19.3	16.4	17.6

NOTES: Myers's Blended Method (Myers, 1940) is applied to calculate the age preference index. The 1971 census data do not provide single-year data for ages above 74. Therefore, in order to compare the pattern of age preference between the 1971 census data and the 1976 NFS household data, we have considered ages 10—69 only in the calculation of age preference.

SOURCES: 1971 census data: Nepal, CBS (1977:61—64). Age structure data for 1976: NFS household data tape.

both sexes probably are still not as smooth as the true age structures, but most of the worst distortions observed in the single-year age reporting are eliminated. Part of our analysis, therefore, is based on these five-year age groups.

Although the grouping of single-year age data into five-year age groups helps to smooth out the erratic single-year age distribution, it does not completely correct for heaping at multiples of five. To overcome this problem, we have used a method developed recently by Feeney (1979). The proportion of ages heaped at each multiple of five is estimated and then the proportion is allocated over the four ages preceding and the four ages following the heaped age. The use of this smoothing technique further reduces the distortion in Nepal's population data caused by age misreporting, as shown in Figure 3.

Table 2 shows the recorded age structure by sex and the age structure after correction for heaping by the Feeney method. Corrections

FIGURE 2 Recorded age distribution of males and females in five-
          year age groups: Nepal, 1976

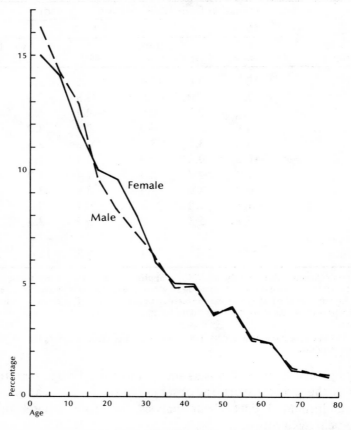

NOTES: The age distributions shown here are based on the NFS household data tape. There
is a slight discrepancy between these data and the data reported in the NFS (Nepal,
FP/MCH Project, 1977:236—37), because some cases were missing from the early data
tape used for that volume. Percentage distributions are based on population for each sex.
SOURCE: NFS household data tape.

are noticeable particularly at ages 15—19 and in the older age groups
40 and over. In this procedure, no adjustments for undercounting by
the NFS have been made. Figure 4 shows the age-sex pyramid of
Nepal corrected for age heaping.

The population pyramid depicted in Figure 4 is wide at the base
and much narrower at the top. This means that Nepal has had a young
population resulting from high fertility. Over 50 percent of the total

FIGURE 3 Age distribution of males and females, corrected for age
misreporting by the Feeney method: Nepal, 1976

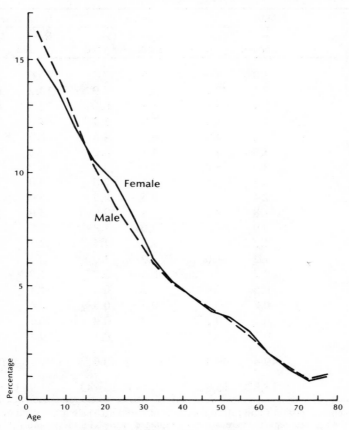

NOTE: Percentage distributions are based on population for each sex.
SOURCES: NFS household data tape and Feeney (1979).

population is under age 20 (Table 2). The surveyed population in 1976
had a sex ratio of 98 males for every hundred females. There were proportionately more females than males in age groups 15–19 through
25–29 and in some older age groups as well. For example, in the ages
20–24, after the recorded male and female ages were smoothed to account for most of the age misreporting, the sex ratio was only 86
males per hundred females, and among people 25–29, the sex ratio
was only 87. The low sex ratio as recorded by the Nepal Fertility Survey may have resulted from migration selective by sex and age.

TABLE 2 Recorded and corrected age distributions (in percentages) of the male, female, and total population: Nepal, 1976

Age groups	Male		Female		Both sexes	
	Re-corded	Cor-rected	Re-corded	Cor-rected	Re-corded	Cor-rected
0—4	8.0	8.0	7.6	7.6	15.6	15.6
5—9	7.1	7.1	7.1	6.9	14.2	14.0
10—14	6.4	6.1	5.9	6.0	12.3	12.1
15—19	4.7	5.0	5.0	5.3	9.8	10.3
20—24	4.0	4.2	4.9	4.8	8.9	9.0
25—29	3.6	3.6	4.1	4.0	7.6	7.7
30—34	3.0	3.0	3.0	3.1	6.0	6.1
35—39	2.4	2.5	2.5	2.6	4.9	5.1
40—44	2.4	2.2	2.5	2.3	5.0	4.5
45—49	1.8	2.0	1.8	2.0	3.6	3.9
50—54	1.9	1.7	2.0	1.8	3.9	3.6
55—59	1.2	1.4	1.3	1.5	2.5	2.9
60—64	1.2	1.0	1.2	1.0	2.4	2.0
65—69	0.7	0.7	0.6	0.7	1.2	1.3
70—74	0.5	0.4	0.5	0.4	1.1	0.9
75—79	0.2	0.2	0.2	0.3	0.4	0.5
80—84	0.2	0.2	0.2	0.2	0.3	0.3
85+	0.1	0.1	0.1	0.1	0.2	0.2
Total %	49.4	49.4	50.5	50.6	99.9	100.0
Total number	15,820	15,820	16,143	16,143	31,963	31,963

NOTES: Percentages may not sum to 100.0 because of rounding. There is a slight discrepancy between the age data reported here and those reported in the NFS First Report (Nepal, FP/MCH Project, 1977:236—37), because some cases were missing from the early data tape used for that volume.

SOURCES: Recorded age distributions: NFS household tape. Corrected age distributions: derived by applying Feeney (1979) method to the recorded age distributions.

POPULATION GROWTH AND AGRICULTURAL PRODUCTION

Table 3 and Figure 5 show Nepal's total population size as recorded in the eight population counts of this century, along with the implied annual intercensal population growth rates. The first census in 1911 was no doubt a serious undercount of the population, but it appears to have been more complete than the subsequent censuses of 1920, 1930, and 1941. Between 1911 and 1954, Nepal's population grew at an

FIGURE 4 Age-sex pyramid of the population of Nepal, 1976

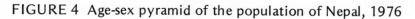

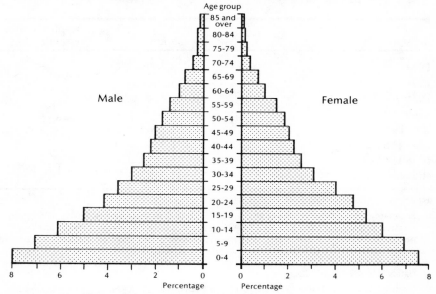

NOTE: The recorded age data are corrected for age misreporting but not adjusted for possible undercounts.

SOURCE: Table 2 (corrected age distributions).

overall average rate of 0.9 percent a year, based on the 1911 and 1954 totals in Table 3. Of course, large annual fluctuations in the population growth rate may have taken place between these years.

The implied annual population growth rates for 1911–20, 1920–30, 1930–41, and 1941–54 from Table 3 should not be taken too seriously, for they may depend more on fluctuating completeness of censuses than on actual growth. It is unlikely that Nepal's population was stationary or declining between 1911 and 1920, although it is possible. There were many Nepalese deaths in the world flu epidemic of 1918 and during World War I, which together could account for a population growth rate somewhat lower than usual. It is also possible that part of the recorded decline in population between 1911 and 1920 is spurious and caused by a worse undercount in 1920 than in 1911.

The apparent decline in population between 1920 and 1930 is also possibly incorrect. The 1930 census was thought to be a particularly bad count:

It is well known that the census of 1930 was deficient owing to a threat of war

TABLE 3 Census totals and implied population growth rates: Nepal,
         1911—76

Reference date	Population	Implied annual growth rate (%)
1911	5,638,749[a]	-0.13
1920	5,573,788[a]	-0.07
1930	5,532,574[a]	1.16
1941	6,283,649[a]	2.20
May 1954	8,361,194[b]	1.78
June 1961	9,471,350[c]	1.99
June 1971	11,555,983[d]	2.10
Midyear 1976	12,837,018[e]	

a   From Nepal, Department of Statistics (1958:4).

b   Estimate derived from census count of people present in their homes in May 1954 in the
    western and central parts of Nepal (4,970,968), plus count of people present in their
    homes in eastern Nepal in May 1952 projected forward two years on the basis of assumed
    growth rates (3,371,493), plus those recorded as absent from their homes but living else-
    where in Nepal (18,733); data and assumed growth rates from Nepal, Department of Sta-
    tistics (1958:1—2, vii, 50).

c   Includes persons at home (9,412,996), from Nepal, CBS (1967: vol. 1, table 1), and per-
    sons absent from home but present in the country (58,354), from Nepal, CBS (1977:12).
    In contrast to the 1952—54 and 1961 censuses, the 1971 census was a modified *de jure*
    count. Persons were counted at their permanent residence if they had been absent for less
    than six months. If they had been absent from home for six months or more but were
    still in Nepal, they were counted where they were living. Thus, the population recorded
    here includes those living in the country and those who had been abroad for less than six
    months. Details on the count are from Nepal, CBS (1977:9—10).

d   From Nepal, CBS (1975a: vol. 1, table 1). Total includes Nepalese who had been living
    abroad for less than six months.

e   From Nepal, CBS (1979:1). Data for 1976 are from the Mid-term Population Sample
    Survey. The sample represented 3.5 percent of the total households in the country. The
    published data refer to the entire population of the country.

between Nepal and Tibet which resulted in a fear among the population that the
census was for the purpose of making up lists for the conscription of men into the
armies (Nepal, Department of Statistics, 1958:vi).

Because the 1930 count was probably too low, the implied population
growth rate of 1.16 percent annually between 1930 and 1941 may be
too high. The implied population growth rate of 2.20 percent a year
between 1941 and 1954, if correct, would have been accounted for
partly by natural population increase and partly by net immigration.
It is also possible that some of the recorded population growth from
1941 to 1952/54 was not genuine, but was due to better coverage of
the population in the later count than in the earlier one.

FIGURE 5 Recorded population growth trends: Nepal census years 1911—76

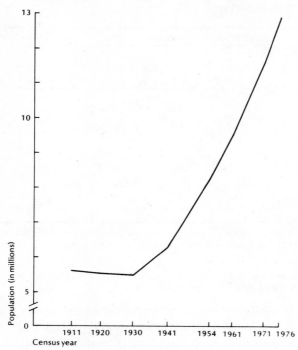

SOURCE: Table 3.

The population growth rates derived from the 1952/54, 1961, and 1971 censuses are in a reasonable range, though they may be somewhat too high if census completeness has been improving. From an average rate of population growth close to 1 percent a year in the first half of this century, the available data indicate that Nepal's population began increasing at about 1.8 percent annually during the 1954—61 period, and then at around 2 percent annually during 1961—71. The sample census of 1976 implies a 1971—76 population growth rate of 2.1 percent per annum. These population counts imply a steadily increasing rate of population growth in recent decades.

An immediate effect of increasing population size is higher population density. During the 1961—71 decade, the population density of Nepal increased by about 23 percent, from 65 to 80 persons per square kilometer. Density varied considerably by geographic area (Table 4).

TABLE 4 Percentage distribution of population, land area, and
         cultivated land area, and density per square kilometer,
         by terrain: Nepal, 1971

| Terrain | Percentage distribution | | | Density per sq. km. | |
	Population	Land area (in sq. kms.)	Cultivated land (in sq. kms.)	Total area	Cultivated area
Mountains	9.8	34.5	4.9	22.7	1,173.8
Hills	47.2	43.5 }	30.4	86.2 }	1,001.9
Kathmandu Valley	5.4	0.7		575.7	
Terai	37.6	21.3	64.8	140.5	336.1
All terrains	100.0	100.0	100.1	na	na
Total number	11,555,983	142,094	19,960	na	na
Total density	na	na	na	80.0	579.0

NOTES: Census land data originally reported in hectares have been converted to square
    kilometers. Percentages may not sum to 100 because of rounding.
na—not applicable.
SOURCES: Data on population and land area are from Nepal, CBS (1975a: vol. 1, table 1).
    Data on cultivated land are as cited by Dhital (1975:99).

With 5.4 percent of the country's population and less than 1 percent
of the land area, Kathmandu Valley, site of the capital, had the highest density—576 persons per sq. km. The mountain terrain, with 9.8
percent of the population and 34.5 percent of the land area, had the
lowest density, owing to its rugged topography. The hill terrain (ex-
cluding Kathmandu Valley) had almost four times the density of the
mountain terrain; and the terai had over six times the density of the
mountains, about 141 persons per sq. km.

In an agricultural and mountainous country like Nepal, a more
meaningful measure of density is the ratio of people to cultivated land
(last column of Table 4). The density per unit of cultivated area in
1971 was more than seven times the density per unit of total land
area. Because the amount of land suitable for cultivation was much
less in the mountains than in the hills or terai, the ratio of population
to cultivated land in the mountains was the highest in the country
(1,174 per sq. km.). In the hills, it was 1,002 per sq. km. and in the
terai only 336. It is evident from Table 4 that the mountain and hill
terrains are facing the greatest population pressure. The population
density per unit of cultivated land has certainly increased since 1971.

As of 1976–77, the average operated land area per rural household was only 0.7 hectare in the hills and 0.6 hectare in the mountains, compared with 1.63 hectares in the terai (Nepal, National Planning Commission Secretariat, 1978:43). Given the marginal nature of much mountain and hill land, whole families or at least some family members must move from the hills and mountains to find arable land or nonagricultural work.

As the rate of population growth has risen, Nepal has faced the difficult problem of increasing its agricultural production to keep up with demand. To assess trends in per capita agricultural production, once again accurate data are needed but not available. There is some doubt about the quality of data even for marketed agricultural products, and much more doubt about data accuracy for farm products consumed by the cultivators. Therefore, any conclusions drawn from these data must be made cautiously.

The United Nations Food and Agriculture Organization (FAO) has compiled available agricultural data for Nepal and constructed an index of the value of total agricultural production over time in constant prices. In Nepal almost all agricultural production consists of foodstuffs. Figure 6 shows Nepal's total and per capita agricultural production for each year of the 1966–77 period, compared with the average agricultural production for the 1961–65 quinquennium. Since 1966, according to the FAO calculations, annual per capita production has been only 85–96 percent of what it was during 1961–65. Because the agricultural sector has accounted for two-thirds of Nepal's gross domestic product in recent years, the failure of agricultural production to keep up with population growth, as had happened by 1966 (Beyer, 1975:82) was a serious matter. FAO indices suggest, however, that from 1966 onward Nepal's agricultural sector has managed to increase production about as fast as population growth. The increase in Nepal's total agricultural production between the crop years 1964–65 and 1976–77 was due almost entirely to the expansion of acreage and labor inputs in the terai (Nepal, Ministry of Food, Agriculture and Irrigation, 1977:7–8, 171). The compilation of agricultural data by Nepal's government suggests a worse picture than that presented in Figure 6. During the period 1964–65 through 1976–77, the total area under major cereal and cash crop cultivation increased by 23 percent, while aggregate reported production of cereal and cash crops (measured in metric tons) increased by only about 15 percent (Nepal, Ministry of

FIGURE 6 Annual total and per capita agricultural production:
Nepal, 1966—77
(Average 1961—65 production = 100)

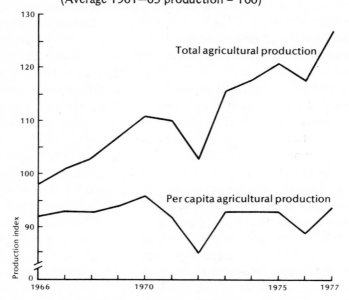

NOTE: The annual index of total agricultural production is a net index; i.e., it is based on net
  production, amounts used for feed and seed having been deducted from the total production figure.
SOURCE: United Nations, FAO (1977:17, 19).

Food, Agriculture and Irrigation, 1977:15—16). Meanwhile Nepal's
total population increased by approximately 28 percent. These data
indicate that crop production increases have fallen substantially behind population growth since the mid-1960s.

Production of Nepal's major crops suffered an overall decline in
yield between 1964—65 and 1976—77. A look at data for individual
crops shows that only one of ten major crops achieved a significant
yield increase during the decade from the mid-1960s to the mid-1970s,
while most had unchanging or slightly declining yields nationwide
(Nepal, Ministry of Food, Agriculture and Irrigation, 1977:15—36).[14]
Paddy rice, by far the country's leading crop in total production and
acreage, had approximately the same yield per hectare in 1974—77 as

14 We compared three-year production averages for 1964—65, 1965—66, and
   1966—67 with averages for 1974—75, 1975—76, and 1976—77 in order to
   smooth out annual fluctuations.

in 1964—67. Maize and wheat, the other leading grain crops, showed slight declines in yields during the decade, as did barley. Substantial declines in yields were reported for potato and tobacco. Modest yield increases were recorded for oilseed, jute, and millet, while a large increase was achieved in sugarcane yields. Some likely causes of the stagnant or declining yields are the increasing erosion of topsoil, the diversion of manure from fertilizer to fuel in response to growing scarcity of firewood, the use of increasingly marginal land for agriculture due to population pressure, and especially the continuing shortage of modern inputs (chemical fertilizer, irrigation, insecticides, improved seeds, agricultural credit) in Nepal's agriculture.

During the Fifth Five-Year Plan period (mid-1975 to mid-1980), the government continued to emphasize the expansion of cultivated land in the terai as a major means of increasing total agricultural production (Nepal, National Planning Commission, 1975:147—8). But unused land suitable for agriculture is running out in the terai. Future agricultural production increases cannot depend on an expansion of acreage, but must be based on the modernization of agricultural production on land already cultivated. Per hectare yields in Nepal are very low by world standards (Shreshtha and Jain, 1978:12). To improve yields, a transformation of agricultural practices and inputs is needed. It is likely that the simple transplantation of "green revolution" agricultural technology from other countries will not prove suitable for Nepal. High-yielding varieties of seeds need to be bred and tested for use there. An appropriate mixture of animal manures, nitrogen-fixing crops, and chemical fertilizers needs to be devised for increasing crop yields. Some suitable combination of biological, ecological, and chemical control of pests is also necessary. Carefully selected mechanical inputs will be needed to increase yields in some of Nepal's cropland, probably beginning with such simple devices as water pumps. Finally, Nepal needs to harness and control its ample water supply for crop irrigation and drainage. Already, families that till irrigated farms usually enjoy much more per capita income and food consumption than farmers whose lands of comparable size are not irrigated (Nepal, National Planning Commission Secretariat, 1978:90—92, 103—4, 139).

Nepal's economy is so heavily dependent on agriculture that the country's poor performance in the agricultural sector is reflected in Nepal's overall economic growth. The World Bank (1976:396) estimated that for the decade of the 1960s, Nepal's gross domestic

product increased 2.5 percent annually. For the Fourth Five-Year
Plan period (mid-1970 to mid-1975), the government and the World
Bank reported an increase of 2.7 percent a year in the GDP. These
economic growth rates for the 1960s and early 1970s were only
slightly higher than Nepal's annual population growth rates. In fact,
taking into account the weak data base for estimates of Nepal's agricultural and total economic performance, there is no certainty that
Nepal's production increases are greater than population growth on a
national basis. The situation in some regions, terrains, and sectors of
the economy may be even worse than on a national scale. Therefore,
Nepal's economy can be characterized as a very slowly developing one
in the aggregate, with virtually constant per capita production.

HEALTH, NUTRITION, AND MORTALITY

As noted earlier, the only comprehensive public health survey available
on Nepal is the Nepal Health Survey (NHS) of 1965—66, which provides an approximate picture of the national public health situation
as of that date. In general, according to the authors of the NHS report,
all of the villages surveyed were characterized by unprotected and contaminated water supplies; lack of sanitary latrines; indiscriminate defe-
cation in public areas; unsanitary food storage, food preparation, and
refuse disposal; deteriorating homes with poor ventilation and severe
crowding; and serious infestation by rats and flies (Worth and Shah,
1969:6—17).

    In spite of the generally unsanitary village environments at that
time, the survey found that the nutritional standard of Nepal's population in the villages surveyed appeared to be adequate (Worth and
Shah, 1969:107). The quantity and variety of food available provided
enough calories for the people, through a predominantly grain diet.
Protein came mostly from several grains combined with beans or len-
tils, with various vegetables, and with occasional high-protein sources
like eggs, meat, or milk from animals (the latter two usually from goats
or cows) owned by almost every rural family. The NHS found no
kwashiorkor or hypo-protein edema in the surveyed villages, which
suggested that severe protein deficiency was not a problem in Nepal
during the mid-1960s (Worth and Shah, 1969:49). The protein situation was precarious, however, with some villages showing very low
protein availability. The urban sample, in general, also reported low
protein intake. Mild deficiencies of Vitamin A, riboflavin, and Vitamin
C were discovered, but deficiency diseases were not widespread.

Several diseases and chronic infections were found by the Nepal Health Survey to be prevalent in Nepal as of the mid-1960s. The iodine-deficiency disease goiter was endemic in certain villages in the hills and mountains. In some villages, as much as 97 percent of the population had goiter, and in most of the villages surveyed, over half of the population was affected by goiter (Worth and Shah, 1969:49—57). The prevalence of deafness and mental retardation was greater in those villages than elsewhere as a result of chronic goiter. The long-term solution to this health problem is relatively simple and inexpensive, requiring the addition of iodine to salt or another food item used by the population. As of the late 1970s, iodine was being added to salt marketed in several regions of Nepal. As the iodine-treated salt becomes a staple in almost all of Nepal's villages, the incidence of goiter should become very low.

During the mid-1960s gonorrhea and syphilis were widespread in Nepal, but both diseases were found to have a low prevalence in most locations. We have no information on whether the incidence of venereal disease has been reduced since 1965—66.

Leprosy remains a serious health problem. Before 1965 the leprosy control program simply tried to isolate infected individuals. Since then the government has attempted to survey populations near health centers to detect afflicted persons, treat the disease, and educate the public about leprosy's cause and treatment (American Public Health Association, 1979:64); but only a tiny proportion of the infected persons is currently being treated.

The Nepal Health Survey found that tuberculosis (TB) was a serious public health problem in urban areas where crowding was great, and to a lesser extent in the villages. Remote areas of the country were still relatively free of tuberculosis as of the mid-1960s, because the disease was not endemic to Nepal. During the 1970s a Tuberculosis Control Project attempted to screen Nepal's entire population for active tuberculosis and to provide BCG immunization to all children under age 15.[15] As of 1978, 55 of Nepal's 75 districts had been covered by mobile TB screening and vaccination teams. Though some problems of implementation remain, it is likely that this project has substantially reduced TB incidence in Nepal.

The NHS found that 72 percent of the children tested in the survey

15 Details of the Tuberculosis Control Project, childhood BCG immunization rates, and TB followup work are found in Vaidya (1979:3.2, 7.8, ch. 11).

villages had intestinal parasites (Worth and Shah, 1969:72—73). The
parasites are passed from person to person through fecal contamina-
tion of water supplies, food, and the entire environment. Parasitic
infections cause loss of full nutritional benefit from food and lowered
resistance to disease. A health survey carried out in one district of the
western hills in 1975 found that diarrhea and gastrointestinal disorders
appeared to be the major causes of death and ill health after the first
month of life. These illnesses are often caused by intestinal parasites
(Nepal, Institute of Medicine, 1975:7—9, 34). The key to eradicating
intestinal parasites lies in improved water supplies and sanitation, and
in basic health education of the populace.

Some polio was found in every village surveyed by the NHS. Ty-
phoid infection was common, and a cholera epidemic had just been
experienced by one of the villages in the sample. Vaccination programs
were minimal during the mid-1960s. This was still true in 1978 (Vaidya,
1979:3.4, 11.26—11.39). Today a critical shortage of almost all kinds
of vaccines and of refrigeration facilities for vaccines is a major handi-
cap of Nepal's preventive health program.

The NHS recorded two successes of Nepal's public health program,
however. The first was a smallpox vaccination program that had
reached most of the adults and teenagers and rather large proportions
of the children surveyed throughout Nepal (Worth and Shah, 1969:
69—71). The program continued during the 1970s. In 1975, Nepal
recorded its last case of smallpox, and in 1977 the country was de-
clared by the World Health Organization to be free of smallpox
(Vaidya, 1979:11.37—11.39). The other success story concerned the
control of malaria during the 1950s and 1960s.

Two main types of malaria had been endemic to Nepal.[16] *P. vivax*
was rather widespread in the terai and inner terai areas. The parasite is
debilitating but not usually fatal, because it attacks only some of the
red blood cells. *P. falciparum* is more virulent and is frequently fatal
because it attacks all the red blood cells of the body. This strain,
which was concentrated in the inner terai valleys at the 300—1,300
meter altitude range, earned them the historical name of "valleys of
death."

In the 1950s, a USAID-sponsored malaria control program began
the spraying of DDT in houses in the malarial areas and at least

---

16 These details on malaria in Nepal are based on personal communication from
   Dr. Robert Worth of the Department of Public Health, University of Hawaii.

temporarily controlled both types of malaria. These traditionally underpopulated areas then became the recipients of large numbers of migrants from the higher altitudes in Nepal. The NHS tested the village populations for malaria and found detectable cases only in the far western terai, though there were indications of recent malarial infections in some eastern terai villages (Worth and Shah, 1969:79–82).

The continuing control of malaria is important for economic development and agricultural production in Nepal. Previously malarial areas now produce about 55 percent of Nepal's total agricultural product (Gaige, 1975:26–28). Unfortunately, there is now a worldwide resurgence of malaria, because malarial mosquitoes are becoming immune to DDT and similar sprays. Therefore, it is likely that malaria is staging a comeback in Nepal as it is elsewhere.[17] A 1975 Nepal government publication reported that the number of malaria victims was increasing at that time (Nepal, National Planning Commission, 1975:504). The number of reported malaria cases in Nepal reached a low of 361 in 1971, then rose to 2,064 in 1972 and rose again to 4,146 in 1973 (American Public Health Association, 1979:24). The resurgence of malaria could be a serious development in the low-altitude terai areas and a devastating occurrence in the inner terai valleys.

Nepal's malaria control program continues today. It is by far the most well-organized, well-funded, adequately staffed, and successful preventive and curative health program in Nepal (Vaidya, 1979: ch. 12). Malaria control workers are supposed to visit each household in their assigned area approximately every month, spraying regularly for mosquitoes and testing any fever victims for malaria. A positive test result should bring a medical worker to the household to administer antimalarial drugs for five successive days. There are some performance problems in the program; some houses are never visited, and about half the persons diagnosed to have active malaria receive less than five days of drug treatment. In spite of these imperfections in implementation of the program, malaria remains reasonably well controlled in Nepal today.

It has been 14 years since the Nepal Health Survey was taken. To our knowledge, there has been no comprehensive national health survey comparable to the NHS since the mid-1960s. A government

---

17 On the recent resurgence of malaria in the Indian subcontinent, and on drugs to control it, see *New York Times* (1977).

description of the public health and medical situation as of 1977 still painted a bleak picture.

... Nepal has made steady progress during the last three economic plans [1961–1975] in raising the health standard of the population. Total expenditure on health activities amounted to 7 percent of total expenditures on economic and social development. Through international cooperation, a malaria eradication programme has successfully been implemented in the Terai area. Cholera and smallpox are no longer threatening epidemics, in spite of the fact that they still toll several hundred souls every year. Malnutrition, measles, tuberculosis and to a major extent intestinal infection and water pollution are still forming a great hazard to the general health of the population. Strenuous efforts in curtailing infectious diseases such as vaccination campaigns and increasing medical personnel are still badly needed. Number of persons per physician is as high as 40,000. Number of hospitals and hospital beds is still far below the adequate level. [In 1971–72 there were 55 hospitals, with total beds numbering 2,006.] The doctor/population ratio in Nepal is the lowest recorded in [the] ESCAP region (Nepal, CBS, 1977:95).

Medical care in 1971–72 was even worse than the aggregate data presented in this quotation suggest, because of the concentration of doctors and hospitals in urban areas and district centers far from where most of the people live. In addition, hospitals were unevenly distributed among regions and terrains, as shown in Table 5. The entire Himalayan mountain section along the northern part of the country had only two small hospitals with a combined capacity of 40 beds, attempting to serve almost 10 percent of Nepal's population, or nearly 28,000 people per bed. The hill areas were relatively well off with 4,638 persons per hospital bed, but hospitals were heavily concentrated in the central hills, whereas other hill areas were poorly served. The terai had only 24 hospitals with a total of 530 beds, but at least transport was somewhat easier there than in the hills or mountains, so that people could reach the nearest hospital by road. The distribution of hospitals and hospital beds by region favored the central region and disadvantaged the eastern and far western regions. As of the late 1970s half of Nepal's districts still had no hospital (American Public Health Association, 1979:1).

The Nepal government has concluded that hospital-based medical care cannot adequately serve the needs of Nepal's scattered population. Small health centers have recently been set up, most of them staffed by paramedical personnel, health aides, and other minimally-trained medical workers. As of 1978, only 21 percent of Nepal's panchayats

TABLE 5 Number and percentage distribution of hospitals and hospital beds in Nepal: June 1971

Hospitals and beds	Nepal total	Terrain distribution			Regional distribution			
		Terai	Hill	Mountain[a]	East	Central	West	Far west
No. of hospitals with ≤ 25 beds	37	18	17	2	8	13	10	6
No. of hospitals with > 25 beds	16	6	10	0	2	9	4	1
Total hospitals	53	24	27	2	10	22	14	7
No. of hospital beds	1,910	530	1,340	40	200	1,230	347	133
% distribution	100.0	27.7	70.2	2.1	10.5	64.4	18.1	7.0
% of total population	100.0	36.6	53.8	9.6	24.2	33.5	21.3	21.0
Total population per hospital bed	6,050	7,986	4,638	27,709	13,988	3,208	7,100	18,250

a One-quarter of the total population of Gorkha District is included in the mountains.

SOURCES: Number of hospitals and beds: compiled from files of the Nepal—University of California Family Planning/Maternal and Child Health Project, University of California, Berkeley, 1976. Population data: Nepal, CBS (1975b: table 1).

had any kind of permanent health facility (Vaidya, 1977:7.9—7.10). The facilities included health posts, family planning clinics, Ayurvedic clinics, and hospitals. Most of them provide medical care free of charge. But the majority of health posts and clinics barely function owing to such problems as inadequate funding, unavailability of trained staff, chronically late salary payments, absenteeism, weak or nonexistent supervision, lack of transport, and severe shortages of equipment, medicines, and vaccines (Vaidya, 1979:3.1—4.5). With more resources and better organization, many of these problems might be overcome. Meanwhile, even in panchayats with health centers, large proportions of the population do not visit them because the centers are inaccessible or inadequate.

The government is now attempting to fill the gap in medical care with village health workers and panchayat-based workers who visit people in their homes. As of 1978, they had visited no more than 30 percent of the country's households even once (Vaidya, 1979:7.6—7.7). These local health workers are minimally trained and carry few medicines. Thus the great majority of Nepal's population is effectively without the benefit of modern medical care. Most people rely on indigenous folk healers and local practitioners of Ayurvedic medicine to treat their illnesses.[18]

The Nepal Nutrition Status Survey of 1975 found nutritional levels to be low in rural Nepal. (The survey, which used anthropometric methods to detect chronic and acute malnutrition among rural children six months to six years old, is described in the section on information sources.) Over 50 percent of the children surveyed were reported to have stunted growth—low height for their age—presumably caused by chronic undernutrition. Higher proportions were found stunted in the hills and the mountains than in the terai (United States, Center for Disease Control, 1975:26—32, 48).

The survey also detected a problem called "wasting," defined operationally as very low weight for the child's height, presumably caused by recent acute undernutrition. Seven percent of the children surveyed showed symptoms of wasting. The prevalence of short-term undernutrition was quite high in the group 6—35 months old but very low among children three to six years old. The problem of low weight for

18 One estimate suggests that over three-fourths of all illnesses in Nepal are treated by the Ayurvedic system of medical care (American Public Health Association, 1979:36).

height among the younger children may indicate that many Nepalese
women have difficulty in providing an adequate supply of breast milk,
that weaning foods are too low in nutritional quality and calories, or
that young children have a low status in the family and do not receive
an adequate portion of food (United States, Center for Disease Control, 1975:45). It is also possible that the feeding of contaminated
food and water to the children starting at about six months causes
systemic infections that prevent them from getting the full nutritional
value from their food.

We noted that the Nepal Health Survey of 1965—66 found generally
adequate nutritional conditions all over Nepal, with certain exceptions
such as the iodine-deficiency disease goiter and low protein consumption among some disadvantaged groups. In contrast, the Nutrition
Status Survey of 1975 concentrated on children in the most suscepti-
ble ages rather than on the whole population and found that 52 percent of them had suffered from long-term undernutrition, 7 percent
were experiencing acute undernutrition at the time of the survey, and
4 percent were in the critical group experiencing both chronic and
acute undernutrition. In addition, the 1975 survey detected a kwashiorkor rate of over 3 percent among the children examined, whereas
the 1965—66 survey had found no kwashiorkor.

Whether these different survey results ten years apart mean that nutritional conditions in Nepal deteriorated in that decade can only be
speculated. During the 1965—75 decade, Nepal experienced rapid population growth. Plots of land that had been barely large enough for a
family became inadequate as the number of mouths to feed increased.
Per capita food intake may have declined in hill and mountain families
whose members did not migrate to the terai in search of new land.
Among those who did migrate, the dislocations caused by the move
may have disrupted food supplies. We would, therefore, not be sur-
prised to learn that nutritional conditions had deteriorated between
1965 and 1975 for a substantial proportion of Nepal's population,
though we lack conclusive evidence that this happened. The Nepal
Health Survey and the Nepal Nutrition Status Survey were so different
in their sample designs, purposes, and methods of measurement that
their results are barely comparable. The approximately constant level
of per capita agricultural production in Nepal since 1966 suggests that
nutritional conditions might also have remained constant. But we have
discovered no usable data indicating whether Nepal's income distribu-

tion or the distribution of access to arable land has worsened, stayed the same, or improved since 1966. Income level and access to land are crucial determinants of the present nutritional status of Nepal's population, because people with the lowest income and without access to land are nutritionally most vulnerable.

Though nutrition trends over time cannot be ascertained, it is clear that a large proportion of Nepal's current population is nutritionally vulnerable. A 1977 national economic survey reported that about 64 percent of the households in its rural sample were landless or tilled marginal or small farms.[19] Income inequality in 1976—77 was severe in rural areas of Nepal; the wealthiest 19 percent of rural families in the survey received 58 percent of rural aggregate net income, whereas the poorest 66 percent of families received only 21 percent of the income. On average, 72 percent of total consumption expenditure in rural households was for food; only 2 percent went for health and education (Nepal, National Planning Commission Secretariat, 1978:35, 123, 135—39).

Recent mortality trends in Nepal are somewhat easier to document than changes in health status. Most mortality estimates for Nepal come from stable or quasi-stable population analysis of census age structures. Because of age misreporting in the data, some sort of smoothing procedure is first done on the ages as reported. Next, an adjustment is made for serious underreporting of children of ages 0—4, and perhaps for obvious underreporting of males or females at other ages as well. Finally, a model stable population is usually chosen from the estimated age structure and estimated population growth rate (see Coale and Demeny, 1966: ch. 1—3). This stable population is characterized by a designated crude death rate and a model life table representing a particular level of mortality.

Various estimates have emerged of Nepal's mortality level at different times. As shown in Table 6, two analyses of the 1952/54 census age structure concluded that the expectation of life at birth in the early 1950s was low, on the order of 28—31 years. There was some improvement in mortality by 1961. Two analyses of the 1961 census age distribution estimated the expectation of life to be about 33 years for females and 30—35 years for males, and the crude death rate to be

---

19 Results of this survey must be interpreted with caution because the sample was not strictly representative of Nepal's total population. The urban population was overrepresented; we therefore report rural results only.

TABLE 6 Mortality estimates for Nepal, from various sources

Year or period	Crude death rate (per 1,000)	Expectation of life at birth (years)		Source	Technique
		Female	Male		
1952/54	37	28.5	27.1	Vaidyanathan and Gaige (1973)	Quasi-stable analysis
1952/54	u	29.4	31.6	Kramer (1979:23)	Arriaga (1968) technique
1961	27	37.4	35.2	Nepal, CBS (1977:85—98)	Stable population analysis
1961	32	33.0	30.2	Krotki and Thakur (1971:91, 97)	Stable population analysis
1961	27	32.5	34.7	Kramer (1979:23)	Arriaga (1968) technique
1965—66	27	u	u	Worth and Shah (1969:27—29)	From reported data on deaths in previous 12 months
1966	28	u	u	Nepal, CBS (1977:78—94)	From 1961—71 survivorship ratios
1971	u	38.9	42.9	Gubhaju (1974)	Quasi-stable analysis
1971	21	39.9	37.0	Nepal, CBS (1977:85—95)	Stable population analysis
1974—76	21	41.8	44.7	Kramer (1979: 7—8)	Based on age-at-death data from 1974—76 Demographic Sample Survey

u—unavailable.

27—32 per thousand. As of 1966 the crude death rate was still 27—28, according to two sources using different techniques of estimation.

Further improvement in Nepal's mortality situation was detected by 1971. Two analyses of the 1971 census age structure concluded that life expectancy had risen to 39—40 years for females and 37—43 years for males. Life tables derived from the Demographic Sample Survey of 1974—76 estimated an expectation of life at birth of 42 years for females and 45 years for males.

These estimates suggest that during the two decades from the early

1950s to the early 1970s, Nepal's expectation of life at birth rose from around 30 years to over 40 years, and the crude death rate declined to slightly over 20 per thousand population. Even after this improvement, Nepal continued to have one of the highest crude death rates and lowest life expectancies in the South and Southeast Asian region.[20]

Another important indicator of the general health and survival chances of a population is the infant mortality rate. It has been difficult to get a reasonably accurate estimate of Nepal's infant mortality rate. Infant and child deaths have been severely underreported in the censuses. The longitudinal Demographic Sample Survey of 1974–78 attempted to collect accurate infant mortality data, but again respondents underreported infant deaths.

So far the only reliable source of information on infant mortality in Nepal is the 1976 Nepal Fertility Survey. The NFS attempted to elicit complete pregnancy histories including the reporting of each infant death and the month of death. Many cross-checking questions were asked of the respondents, in order to maximize the completeness of reporting. Comparison of NFS data on infant mortality with other sources of information demonstrates that the NFS contains the most complete reporting of infant mortality of any census or survey in Nepal to date (see Goldman et al., 1979:35–39, tables 17–19).[21]

Thapa and Retherford (forthcoming) have analyzed the levels, trends, and differentials of infant mortality in Nepal based on the 1976 Nepal Fertility Survey. Infant mortality rates by mothers' ages for the 1970–74 period (Table 7) show an expected U-shaped relationship; infant mortality is highest for young mothers, the low plateau is among women of ages 30–39, and the rate rises again for older mothers. The infant mortality rate for all ages during 1970–74 was 156 per thousand live births.

Infant mortality rates prior to 1960 were found to be substantially underreported (Thapa and Retherford, forthcoming). In Table 8, we present the infant mortality rates for 1960–74 for the three major terrains as well as for the whole country. The estimates show that the

---

20 For comparative mortality data, including data on infant mortality in South and Southeast Asia, see Vernon (1980) and United Nations, ECAFE (n.d.).

21 Evaluation of World Fertility Survey data for several other countries has also shown that the coverage and accuracy of reporting of infant and child mortality data were surprisingly good. Thus, "the World Fertility Survey data can be used with confidence to estimate the current level and recent trend in infant and child mortality" (Chidambaram et al., 1980:35).

TABLE 7 Infant mortality rates for births classified by age of mother: Nepal, 1970—74

Mothers' ages	No. of infant deaths per 1,000 live births
15—19	213
20—24	163
25—29	142
30—34	129
35—39	125
40—44	145
All ages	156

NOTE: Births to mothers below age 15 are included in births to mothers aged 15—19, and births to mothers aged 45—49 are included in births to mothers aged 40—44.

SOURCE: Thapa and Retherford (forthcoming: table 3).

national infant mortality rate fell from 182 to 168, a decline of 14 per thousand live births, between 1960—64 and 1965—69. Between 1965—69 and 1970—74, the infant mortality rate declined from 168 to 156, a 12 point drop. There was an average of almost a 3 point decline in infant mortality per year during 1960—74 in Nepal. Table 8 also shows that there have been startling differences in infant mortality levels and trends over time for the terrains of the country. The mountains had vastly higher infant mortality than the hills.[22] Infant mortality in the terai, though not quite so high as that in the mountains, also remained considerably higher than that of the hills. The

TABLE 8 Infant mortality rates by terrain: Nepal, 1960—74

Period	No. of infant deaths per 1,000 live births			
	Mountain	Hill	Terai	Total country
1960—64	238	150	212	182
1965—69	189	149	183	168
1970—74	188	143	165	156

NOTE: The rates presented here are adjusted for age heaping and corrected for age truncation. (For details see Thapa and Retherford, forthcoming.)

SOURCE: Thapa and Retherford (forthcoming: tables 1 and 12).

---

22 Because of the smaller sample size, rates for the mountain region are subject to greater sampling error than those for the other two regions.

differentials are not surprising, in part because the hills may be a more healthful environment than the hot, moist, malarial terai or the rugged and harsh mountains. The hills also have an advantage in the number of hospital facilities per capita, and they may have developed better clinic facilities than the other two regions (see Table 5). More research is needed to pin down the size of the infant mortality differentials between the terrains and the reasons for such differentials.

Analysis of NFS data shows that short spacing between births is correlated with high infant mortality (Thapa and Retherford, forthcoming: table 8). The longer the time between births, the lower is the probability of the death of the infant born at the end of the interval. For instance, during the period 1970–74, infants born less than two years after their mother's previous birth had an infant mortality rate of 213. Those born two to three years after the previous live birth had an infant mortality rate of 143. Children born after a birth interval of three years or more had an infant mortality rate of 86. These findings suggest that lengthening birth intervals in Nepal could contribute to reducing infant mortality.

It is clear from the data presented here that the infant mortality level in Nepal, still 156 infant deaths per thousand live births in the early 1970s, was high by any standard. In addition, the available evidence indicates that Nepal's overall crude death rate by the mid-1970s was still over 20 deaths per thousand population per year, which is considered a high death rate even among developing countries. During the late 1970s, the government's attempts to lower mortality focused on the high altitude areas where the worst mortality situation prevailed. The Fifth Five-Year Plan (mid-1975 to mid-1980) envisaged the setting up of one clinic per 5,000 people in the mountains during the plan period (Nepal, National Planning Commission, 1975:503–4). These clinics were to be responsible primarily for family planning, maternal and child health work, and immunizations. If the projected number of mountain clinics was established and staffed, this would help to narrow the mortality gap between the mountains and the other two terrains of Nepal.

By historical standards, Nepal has made substantial gains in the control of morbidity and mortality, but in comparison with many other less developed countries, Nepal's achievements have been modest. Part of the problem may be that per capita expenditures on public health and curative health care remain very low. In 1974 the World

Health Organization estimated that combined public and private health expenditures in Nepal were about 24 rupees per capita per year (approximately US $2.00) with about four-fifths of this amount spent in the private sector (American Public Health Association, 1979:32a). The other urgent problem is that basic preventive and primary health care in Nepal has not reached most of the villages. Until it does, gains in the control of disease, infant mortality, and overall mortality will be slow.

NUPTIALITY

Nepal has a pattern of early and universal marriage for both males and females. Child marriage used to be customary and still exists to some extent, particularly in the remote rural areas. Marriage may begin before age ten for either partner, in matches arranged by parents. As of 1971, 1 percent of boys and 2 percent of girls in the 6—9 age group were already formally married (Table 9). Proportions ever married rose to 6 percent for boys and 13 percent for girls among those 10—14 years old. Married children, however, may not begin living together as husband and wife until about the time of the girl's menarche. As a rule she then moves in with her husband's family, and the "effective marriage" begins. The teenage couple may remain subfecund for several years after their effective marriage starts, though, and not have their first child until the wife is 17 or older. Thus reducing child marriage in Nepal may have little direct effect on fertility levels.

The censuses of Nepal provide data on the formal marriage age of males and females. Using the census data we can calculate singulate mean age at marriage (SMAM). Comparing males and females as of 1961 or 1971, it is clear from Table 9 that girls generally marry at younger ages than boys, which implies that it is customary for females to marry males several years (about four years on the average) older than themselves. Almost every male and female eventually marries in Nepal, and both sexes start marrying at a very young age; but females marry at a much faster rate than males. Males begin marrying at a lower age in Nepal than in any other East Asian, South Asian, or Southeast Asian country; and females begin marrying earlier in Nepal and India than in any of the other countries of those regions.[23]

---

23 Smith (1978) has calculated nuptiality indicators for most Asian countries, based on census data. Using Coale's (1971) three-parameter model of nuptiality, Smith reports the following figures for Nepal: a_0, the age at which

TABLE 9 Percentages of males and females ever formally married: Nepal, 1952—76

Age group	Males 1952/54 census	1961 census	1971 census	1976 NFS	Females 1952/54 census	1961 census	1971 census	1976 NFS
6—9	u	3.0	1.2	u	u	5.3	2.4	u
10—14	12.2	10.7	6.3	u	28.8	24.9	13.4	u
15—19	u	36.6	27.0	26.8	u	73.9	60.7	62.7
20—24	u	73.2	66.9	67.2	u	94.6	92.1	94.0
25—29	u	89.7	87.7	91.2	u	98.1	97.4	98.2
30—34	u˙	95.2	94.4	96.8	u	99.0	98.6	98.8
35—39	u	97.3	96.8	98.0	u	99.2	98.9	99.4
40—44	u	97.9	97.7	98.7	u	99.3	99.1	99.5
45—49	u	98.4	98.4	98.9	u	99.4	99.2	99.3
50—54	u	98.5	98.6	u	u	99.5	99.3	u
55—59	u	98.7	98.8	u	u	99.5	99.3	u
Singulate mean age at marriage[a]	u	19.5	20.8	20.8	u	15.2	16.7	17.2

u—unavailable.

a The standard calculation for singulate mean age at marriage (SMAM) assumes that no one marries before age 15. For the 1961 and 1971 censuses of Nepal, we have used the following version of the formula, which assumes that no one marries before age 6:

$$SMAM = \frac{600 + 4 \, _4s_6 + 5(\sum_{x=10}^{45} \, _5s_x) - (50 \, s_{50})}{100 - s_{50}}$$

where s_x is the percentage single at age x. SMAM is equivalent to the mean number of years spent in the single (never married) state by those in the hypothetical cohort who marry by age 50. (See Hajnal, 1953:129—30; and Smith, 1978:2.)

SOURCES: 1952—54: Nepal, Department of Statistics (1958:35). 1961 and 1971: Nepal, CBS (1977:104—5). 1976: NFS household data tape.

Comparing the census data in Table 9 over time, it is clear that both male and female formal marriage ages rose between 1961 and 1971. The only comparable data from the published 1952/54 census results indicate that formal marriage ages also rose between 1952/54 and

significant numbers of a cohort begin to enter marriage, was age 10.5 for males and 10.0 for females, based on 1971 census data. *C*, the maximum percentage ever married in a cohort, was 98.4 for males and 99.2 for females. *k*, an index of tempo of marriage, was high for males—.906—signifying a slow process of marriage in a cohort, and was low for females—.596—indicating a rather fast tempo of marriage once a cohort begins marrying. See also Smith (1980).

1961. The proportion of males in the 10–14 age group who were reported as ever married declined from 12.2 percent in 1952/54 to 10.7 percent in 1961 and further to 6.3 percent in 1971. Similarly, the proportion of females aged 10–14 who were ever married declined from 28.8 percent in 1952/54 to 24.9 percent in 1961 and further to 13.4 percent in 1971. In this age group, the change for both sexes was much greater during 1961–71 than during 1952/54–61, which suggests that formal marriage ages were rising slowly during the 1950s and faster during the 1960s.

Age at marriage has been rising all over Asia in recent decades (Smith, 1980). The reasons for the rise in Nepal are not clear. A 1962 law setting minimum marriage ages of 14 years for females and 18 years for males may have affected the timing of some marriages; a later revision changed the minimum ages to 16 and 18 years respectively, with parental consent. Without parental consent, the minimum ages are now 18 for females and 21 for males (Nepal, CBS, 1977:102). Though this law may have had some effect in discouraging child marriages, it is unenforceable owing to the lack of birth and marriage registration in many areas. Because of the existence of the law, some of the recently reported rise in marriage age may be spurious. Proportions married at the younger ages may be slightly underreported because some respondents might intentionally misreport the marital status of their children.

The two most recent censuses provided data on current marital status that showed differences in marriage age for various groups (Nepal, CBS, 1977:104–5). The 1961 census showed that literate females married much later than illiterate females, whereas literate males married slightly earlier than illiterate males. Urban people of both sexes married much later than rural people, as we would expect. Marriage data from the 1971 census differentiated respondents by terrain. Formal marriages occurred at much earlier ages in the terai than in any other part of Nepal. In the terai as of 1971, the female singulate mean age at marriage was only 15.02 years and the male SMAM was 19.45, considerably lower than Nepal's national averages for 1971.[24] The data suggest that the incidence of child marriage is much higher in the terai than elsewhere in Nepal. In contrast, people of the mountains, particularly the women, reported higher marriage ages than inhabitants of the

[24] The Baseline KAP Survey of 1975 also found that terai women married much earlier than hill women (Tuladhar et al., 1978:23–24).

other two terrains. The reasons for the differentials still remain
speculative. One factor may be religion. The 1976 Nepal Fertility Survey found that the mean age at marriage for Buddhist women (17.1
years) was markedly higher than the mean for Hindu women (15.0
years) and Muslim women (14.2 years). (See Nepal, FP/MCH Project,
1977:37.)

Whether the trend of a rising formal marriage age has continued
since 1971 is not clear. NFS data suggest little or no change between
1971 and 1976 (Table 9). They indicate slightly higher proportions
of males and females ever married in most age groups than reported
by the 1971 census. This slight disparity may be due to the greater
degree of probing in the survey than in the census or to sampling error
in the survey.

One obvious reason why many developing country governments are
interested in raising the age at marriage is that this can reduce fertility
even without widespread contraceptive use. Higher marriage ages, especially for females, can contribute to a reduction of fertility by
lengthening the time between successive generations, lowering the
number of fecund years that couples are married, and giving young
people time to develop other life choices besides having large families.

The fertility effects of a rising marriage age depend in part on the
previous fertility of the affected age groups. The NFS data show that
the fertility of couples in the first five years of marriage is very low if
the wives' effective marriage age is under 15 years. Even if women
marry at ages 15—19, births during the first five years of marriage are
surprisingly few, given that these women and their husbands should
have relatively high fecundity.

Table 10 shows that women surveyed by the NFS who had married
at relatively young ages during the five to nine years preceding the
survey had low fertility during the first five years of marriage. The
retrospective NFS data may not, however, be entirely accurate. Some
of the women who reported a birth before the date of marriage, for
example, may have been reporting a birth from a prior marriage or
may have simply made an error in their reported marriage age and date
(see Goldman et al., 1979:7—11). Among women whose "effective
marriage" began before age 15, 50.3 percent did not give birth during
the first five years of effective marriage. For those who did experience
a childbirth during the first five years of their effective marriages, the
first birth did not occur, on the average, until after 2.7 years of mar-

TABLE 10 Percentages of NFS women married before age 25 who
had first birth during first five years of marriage: NFS,
1976

Timing of first birth	Age at marriage		
	15	15–19	20–24
Before marriage	.0	.4	5.8
< 1 year of marriage	.6	3.5	8.3
1–2 years	7.2	20.8	24.8
2–3 years	13.3	26.3	21.5
3–4 years	15.3	18.0	17.4
4–5 years	13.3	8.1	5.8
Mean number of years	2.7	2.1	1.8
% who had no birth in five years	50.3	23.0	16.5

NOTE: Effective marriages of these NFS respondents took place between midyear 1966 and
midyear 1971. "Effective marriage" means that the wife was formally married, had begun
living with her husband, and had begun menstruating. Mean number of births refers only
to women who gave birth during the first five years of marriage

SOURCE: Nepal, FP/MCH Project (1977:104).

riage. For women whose effective marriages began in the late teens, at
ages 15–19, the surprisingly high proportion of 23.0 percent reported
no birth during the first five years of marriage; and first births that did
occur within five years happened a little more quickly than for
younger women—2.1 years after marriage, on the average. For women
who married at ages 20–24, 16.5 percent had no birth in the first five
years of marriage; but for those who had a birth, the mean interval was
only 1.8 years, or even less if births reported to have occurred before
marriage are assumed to have actually occurred very early in the marriage.

The NFS data suggest that the abolition of marriage among females
under age 15 would have little effect on Nepal's fertility level, because
proportionately few females enter effective marriage before age 15
and, among those who do, fertility during the first five years of marriage is so low. In contrast, a sizable reduction in the proportion married at ages 15–19 could have a considerable negative effect on Nepal's
fertility level. As of 1976, 61.5 percent of females in that age group
were formally married, and a slightly lower proportion were living in
effective marriages (Nepal, FP/MCH Project, 1977:241). Though their
fertility in the first five years of effective marriage was not so high as

might be expected, it was high enough to represent numerous births
that could be postponed or prevented through delayed marriage.

Achieving significant increases in marriage age will not be easy, however. Girls, in particular, need to have other options besides early marriage. One incentive to delay marriage would be the possibility of
more secondary or higher education. Another would be opportunities
for remunerative employment. These changes, where feasible, could
contribute to producing a gradual rise in marriage age.

To raise Nepal's current legal minimum marriage age of 16 for girls
and 18 for boys to some higher ages would probably be ineffective in
the present context. For the current law to be enforced throughout
the country, birth registration will have to be in effect for some time
so that authorities know the age of marriage applicants. The government will have to require the registration of marriages, and village-level
authorities will have to be trained in vital registration work, funded to
do the work, and required to report the results. Meanwhile, much educational effort will be needed to persuade people to postpone their
children's or their own marriages.

Other changes in marriage patterns are beginning to occur that will
have the opposite tendency of increasing fertility. One is an increase
in the remarriage of widows. Traditionally, among the 89 percent of
Nepal's population that is Hindu, the remarriage of widows was forbidden, although the remarriage of widowers was not. The 1962 marriage law legalized the remarriage of widows, but custom still prevents
many widows from remarrying. Therefore, whenever a woman's or
girl's husband dies, her childbearing usually terminates. Widowhood
during a woman's peak childbearing years is not an uncommon occurrence in a country, like Nepal, with high mortality. As the remarriage
of widows becomes more acceptable, widowed women will remarry,
resume childbearing, and thus increase their completed fertility. Meanwhile, the current decline in early widowhood is having the effect of
lengthening the proportion of women's fecund lives spent in the married state. For example, the proportion widowed among women of
ages 30–34 declined from 6 percent in 1961 to about 3 percent in the
early 1970s, and the proportion widowed among women aged 35–39
declined from 12 percent to approximately 7 percent in the same
period (Nepal, CBS, 1977:103). Stoeckel et al.'s (1976) analysis shows
that the decline in widowhood could also contribute to raising Nepal's
crude birth rate, thus neutralizing the simultaneous fertility-reducing

effects of the rising age at marriage. If mortality in Nepal continues to decline, we can expect the incidence of widowhood to decline further as well; and that will tend to increase fertility, particularly in the female age groups 30—34 and above.

Another possible change that could increase fertility in Nepal is earlier menarche. Ever married women interviewed in the NFS reported an average age at first menstruation of 15.1 years and a median age of 15.5 years. It should be noted, however, that the reported age at menarche may have been affected by misreporting. If the rather high reported age at menarche is correct, it probably reflects in part the poor health and nutritional level of Nepal's female population in the decades prior to 1976. When the nutrition of girls improves considerably, and their general health also improves, we can expect a decline in age at menarche followed by a general increase in fecundity after the first menstruation (Frisch, 1978). If teenage marriage is still common at that time, many effective marriages may begin earlier because menstruation begins earlier. In addition, fertility in the first five years of effective marriage could rise, owing to the higher fecundity in a better nourished population, unless it is countered by the use of contraception in early marriage.

As menarche comes earlier, as fecundity rises, as the incidence of widowhood declines, and as more widows remarry, fertility in Nepal will tend to increase unless compensating changes take place. One such change would be a significant rise in marriage ages, which would both postpone childbearing and reduce the number of years during which women would be exposed to childbearing. Another compensating change would be a reduction in marital fertility through increased use of contraception and abortion, both for spacing births and for terminating childbearing.

FERTILITY

The two most recent censuses of Nepal asked for information on fertility. The 1961 census asked how many children each woman had ever borne. The replies referred to women's fertility experience in the decades from the 1920s through the 1950s. As shown in Table 11, parities reported in 1961 increased with each successive age group of women, a pattern we would expect; but the women of ages 45—49 in 1961 reported an average completed parity of only 4.93 children, which is lower than the average completed parity reported by women

TABLE 11   Reported number of children ever born per woman:
1961 and 1971 censuses and 1976 Nepal Fertility Survey

Age group of women	1961	1971	1976
15—19	.23	.16	.20
20—24	1.32	1.01	1.35
25—29	2.45	2.11	2.85
30—34	3.74	3.04	4.05
35—39	4.18	3.67	5.04
40—44	4.75	3.93	5.50
45—49	4.93	3.97	5.70

NOTE: 1961 and 1971 parities were calculated from census data on the number of women in
each age group (unadjusted for age misreporting or underenumeration) and on the number
of children ever born reported by these women. The 1976 NFS collected data on parity
from ever married women only. Therefore, to calculate number of children ever born for
1976, we divided the number of ever married women in each age group by the proportion
of women in that age group who had ever married, calculated from the NFS Household
Survey, in order to obtain an estimate of the total number of women in each age group.

SOURCES: 1961: Nepal, CBS (1977:113). 1971: Nepal, CBS (1975a: vol. 4, table 32; 1977:
117). 1976: NFS individual and household data tapes.

aged 45—49 in 1976. This could indicate that fertility was underreported in the 1961 census. It is also possible that women in the early
part of the century had an average of only five births, even though
they all married at a young age. Recent research has shown that some
Asian cultures in the past combined early and universal marriage with
only moderate levels of completed fertility, on the order of five to six
children per woman. The agricultural population of China in 1930,
for example, exhibited such a pattern of universal marriage and moderate fertility (Barclay et al., 1976). Thus, 1961 census data on number of children ever born in Nepal should not be completely dis-
counted.

The 1971 census asked women how many children they had ever
borne, and also asked them about births during the previous year. The
reporting of children ever born appears to have been less accurate in
that census than in the 1961 census. At all ages, reported parity was
much lower for 1971 than for 1961. For example, women who were
45—49 in 1971 reported an average completed fertility of only 3.97
children, but ten years earlier the same cohort had reported having
borne an average of 4.18 children by ages 35—39. Similarly, the reporting of births in the year prior to the 1971 census was very low for

all ages. A total fertility rate of only 3.21 children per woman comes from the recorded 1971 census data on number of births during the previous year.[25] To adjust data on births last year by reported parities we have used a standard demographic technique described in National Academy of Sciences (1979:3-20 to 3-32). This results in an adjusted total fertility rate of 5.41 children per woman in 1970—71. The fertility estimates based on 1971 census fertility questions should be treated with caution, however, because the components of these estimates are so inadequate.

Several surveys besides the NFS have attempted to estimate fertility levels in Nepal. The Nepal Health Survey of 1965 asked ever married women about current and recent pregnancies, how many births there had been in the household during the previous 12 months, and how many live births they had had altogether. Most of the resulting compilations are not currently available. Worth and Shah (1969:18—25) estimated a crude birth rate of 50—55 per thousand population, which is probably too high for Nepal at that time, and a total fertility rate of 6.5 children per woman.

A decade later, the longitudinal Demographic Sample Surveys of 1974—75, 1976, and 1977—78 attempted to reinterview households every six months and record all the births in each interval. Recorded data from the first interviews and the first round of reinterviews (1974—75) yielded a total fertility rate (TFR) of 3.21 children per woman for urban areas and 5.42 for rural areas, for a national TFR of 5.33 (Bourini, 1976:20—21, 33). These raw data were inflated by a correction factor derived from a small postenumeration matching survey to give an estimated national TFR of 6.26 children per woman. (For a discussion of the derivation of this correction factor, see the section on sources of information on Nepal's population.) Unadjusted data from the 1976 reinterviews gave an urban TFR of 3.63 and a rural TFR of 5.59, which together produced an estimated TFR of 5.51 for Nepal in 1976 (Bourini, 1977:10—12, 22). Again the raw data were inflated to give an estimated TFR of 6.41 for the country. Finally, the last round of interviews in 1977—78 produced an unadjusted TFR of 3.33 for urban areas and 5.37 for rural areas, or 5.29 for all Nepal (Nepal, CBS,

---

25 Data on male and female births during the year preceding the census and unadjusted data on women in each age group are from Nepal, CBS (1975a: vol. 4, table 32). Births to women under age 15 are allocated to the 15—19 age group, and births to women of ages 50 and over are allocated to the 45—49 age group.

1977:2—3, 17). This was adjusted to a TFR of 6.24 for the country. These DSS data on fertility are rather weak, especially as the surveys were not fully representative of the nation as a whole.

Table 11 also presents data on children ever born from the Nepal Fertility Survey. At almost all ages, women interviewed by the NFS in 1976 reported having had more births than had been reported for women of the same age group in the 1961 census. This means either that the fertility level was lower during the decades prior to 1961 than it was during 1961—76, or that fertility had been underreported in the 1961 census. A rise in fertility would have been possible, if diseases and customs that had regulated fertility before 1961 were controlled or changed during the 1960s.

Table 12 shows mean number of children ever born by age group of women calculated from NFS data for the three terrains of Nepal as of 1976. At every age group through ages 40—44 women of the terai reported having experienced more births than women of the same age in the hills, and women of the hills reported more births than women of corresponding age in the mountains. This finding is consistent with female age at marriage being lowest in the terai and highest in the mountains. Fertility data from women in the oldest age group (45—49), however, indicate that both mountain and hill women reported an average completed parity of about six births. These data may be accurate, but in general NFS data from the mountains are less reliable than data from the hills and the terai because they are subject to greater sampling error due to small sample size.

Terai women of ages 45—49 reported fewer children ever born than did hill or mountain women of the same ages or terai women in the 40—44 age group. If we assumed that terai women in the 45—49 age group simply underreported their completed fertility, by forgetting to report the births of some children who died or by forgetting to report the existence of grown children, we would estimate that they had an actual completed parity of six or slightly more births per woman. Indeed, the low reported parity may have resulted from underreporting. But it is also possible that these women actually experienced reduced parity as a result of having suffered from malaria during their peak childbearing years. As we have already reported, malaria was not brought under control in Nepal until the late 1950s. Data from Sri Lanka support the hypothesis that malaria reduces a population's fertility. In Sri Lanka after malaria control, all previously malarial areas

TABLE 12 Mean number of children ever born per woman, by
terrain: 1976 Nepal Fertility Survey

Age group of women	Terai	Hills	Mountains
15—19	.30	.16	.11
20—24	1.44	1.32	1.08
25—29	3.07	2.72	2.38
30—34	4.29	4.01	3.24
35—39	5.15	5.03	4.63
40—44	5.73	5.48	5.04
45—49	5.24	5.99	6.00

NOTE: To calculate number of children ever born, we divided the number of ever married
women in each age group by the proportion of women in that age group who had ever
married, calculated from the NFS Household Survey, in order to obtain an estimate of the
total number of women in each age group.
SOURCE: Calculated from NFS individual and household data tapes.

experienced sharply rising birth rates, but nonmalarial areas in Sri
Lanka did not (Fuller et al., 1980:8—11; Ratnayake and Fuller, 1980:
7—13, table 4). If malaria had a similar depressant effect on fertility
in Nepal's terai, fertility among terai women would have begun rising
after the malaria control program began in the 1950s. By the time of
the 1976 NFS, cohorts of women up through ages 25—29 would not
have been affected by malaria during their childbearing years, and the
age cohorts of 30—34 through 40—44 would have experienced enough
fecund years after malaria control to make up for reduced fertility in
their earlier childbearing years. Terai women of ages 45—49 in 1976,
however, had been in their early thirties as malaria control spread in
the terai; perhaps they were not able to make up completely for earlier reduced childbearing. The birth history data from the NFS support
the hypothesis that terai women experienced lower fertility than expected during their early childbearing years, and higher fertility than
expected during their later childbearing years.

From the NFS birth histories of respondents for the three quin-
quennia prior to 1976, it has been possible to estimate age-specific fertility rates for Nepal (Table 13). We have made no adjustments for
possible underreporting of births or for misreporting of the ages of
mothers or children. Only ever married women between the ages of 15
and 49 in 1976 were interviewed, and therefore age-specific fertility
data are unavailable for the older age groups in the earlier years. For

The Population Dynamics of Nepal

TABLE 13 Age-specific fertility rates: Nepal, 1961—75
(Rates per thousand women)

Age group	1961—65	1966—70	1971—75
15—19	134	139	135
20—24	260	275	281
25—29	281	296	291
30—34	243	248	236
35—39	u	183	167
40—44	u	u	85
45—49	u	u	(15)
CFR	4,593	4,793	4,719
TFR	u	u	6,055

NOTES: In the calculation of rates shown in the table, the number of ever married women in each age group was divided by the proportion of women in that age group who had ever married, estimated from the NFS Household Survey, in order to obtain an estimate of the total number of women in each age group.

Each age-specific fertility rate shown in the table is an annual rate averaged over a five-year period to minimize annual fluctuations from age misreporting. For example, the first entry in the table means that out of 1,000 females aged 15—19, on average 134 of them had a birth in any given year during the period 1961—65.

CFRs and TFRs are calculated from values more exact than the rounded age-specific fertility rates shown in the table.

The rate in parentheses indicates a slight truncation. For instance, women who were 49 years of age in 1975 were only 45 in 1971. Because of this, no data are available on women who would have been 46, 47, 48, or 49 in the year 1971. However, since the fertility of women of these ages is not great, the rates should not be biased considerably. If the rate for an age group were biased, it would be biased upward. Therefore, the TFR calculated from birth histories for the period 1971—75 could not be biased downward.

u—not available because of age truncation.

CFR—cumulative fertility rates up to age 35.

TFR—total fertility rates.

SOURCE: Calculated from NFS individual and household data tapes.

instance, the fertility history data for the year 1967 refer to females who were between ages six and 40 at that time, and there is no fertility information about women who were then 41—49.

The rates presented in Table 13 suggest a slight rise in fertility in all age groups between 1961—65 and 1966—70, and a slight decline in fertility in most age groups between 1966—70 and 1971—75. The changes are so minor, however, that they could easily be due to age misreporting of women and children, or to a small number of omitted births. Figure 7, which presents the period cumulative fertility rate (CFR) for women below age 35 for each of the 15 years prior to the

FIGURE 7 Cumulative fertility rates up to age 35 in single years: Nepal, 1961—75

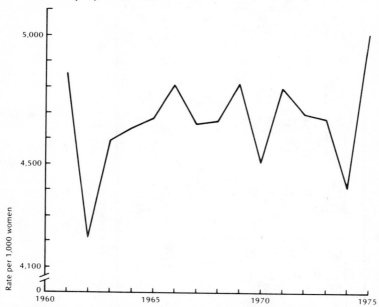

NOTE: Rates refer to all women—both ever married and never married. The number of ever married women at each age is divided by the proportion of ever married women at that age, calculated from NFS data, in order to estimate the total number of women at each age.

SOURCE: NFS individual and household data tapes.

survey, reveals that reported cumulative fertility fluctuated between 4.2 and 5.0 births per woman with no strong rising or declining fertility trend. We therefore conclude that, during the period 1961—75, there was no consistent fertility trend among Nepalese women under age 35.

Data for the 1971—75 period add up to a total fertility rate (TFR) of about 6.1 births per woman for all Nepal. Birth data for the 12 months prior to the NFS indicate a TFR of about 6.2 to 6.3 for the 1975—76 period (see Goldman et al., 1979:21, 35). These differences are too small to indicate any trend. Therefore, from the NFS data we estimate that during the early and mid-1970s Nepal had a total fertility rate of about 6.1 to 6.3 births per woman. As far as we can tell from NFS data for the country as a whole, Nepal experienced no change in its TFR during the 1961—76 period.

TABLE 14 Age-specific fertility rates by terrain: Nepal, 1961–75
(Rates per thousand women)

Age group	Terai			Hills			Mountains		
	1961–65	1966–70	1971–75	1961–65	1966–70	1971–75	1961–65	1966–70	1971–75
15–19	151	166	163	127	124	120	89	85	90
20–24	261	285	295	266	271	277	231	261	238
25–29	270	313	310	293	285	279	249	290	273
30–34	229	245	232	260	254	245	216	218	203
35–39	u	176	153	u	191	174	u	164	170
40–44	u	u	83	u	u	82	u	u	121
45–49	u	u	(8)	u	u	(18)	u	u	(30)
CFR	4,556	5,043	5,002	4,729	4,670	4,610	3,927	4,268	4,022
TFR	u	u	6,219	u	u	5,978	u	u	5,930

NOTE: See Table 13 for explanation of how rates were calculated and the values in parentheses.
u–not available because of age truncation.
CFR–cumulative fertility rates up to age 35.
TFR–total fertility rates.
SOURCE: Calculated from NFS individual and household data tapes.

Age-specific fertility rates for the three terrains indicate only minor fertility differentials during the most recent period, 1971—75, adding up to a total fertility rate of 6.2 births per woman in the terai, 6.0 in the hills, and 5.9 in the mountains (Table 14). As can be seen from

FIGURE 8 Age-specific fertility rates by terrain: Nepal, 1971—75

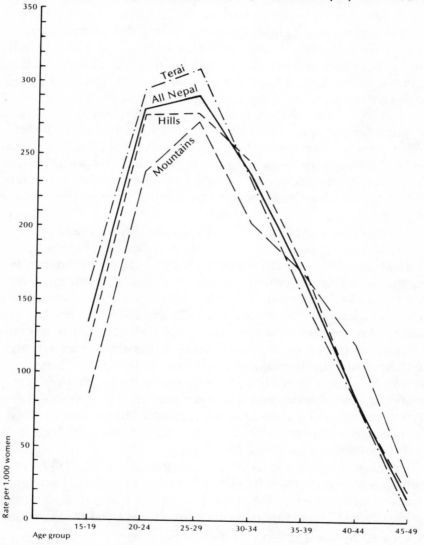

SOURCE: Tables 13 and 14.

Figure 8, Nepal's terai and hills display a broad peak fertility pattern, with high fertility in both the 20—24 and 25—29 age groups; but the mountains show a late peak fertility pattern, with the highest age-specific fertility concentrated in the 25—29 age group.[26] In the terai, women began childbearing very early and had high fertility at ages 15—29, but their fertility began declining more sharply and at earlier ages than in the other terrains. Women of the hills began their childbearing slightly later than in the terai, and did not experience quite so high a fertility level as terai women during ages 20—29. But hill women continued bearing children at older ages to a greater degree than terai women. Mountain women married and began childbearing comparatively late, achieving lower age-specific fertility at ages 15—24 than women in the other two terrains. But they reported a much older reproductive pattern, continuing to have children in their forties at higher rates than women of the hills and terai. Thus, though cumulative fertility rates up to age 35 show marked differentials by terrain, the hill and mountain women experienced almost as high a total fertility rate as terai women through a later childbearing pattern than in the terai.

What fertility trends are evident by terrain? The hill women reported steady fertility for the 1961—75 period; no pronounced changes can be documented for any age group. Mountain women reported a slight rise in fertility, especially in the 20—29 age span, between 1961—65 and 1966—70, and a slight decline in fertility among women of ages 20—34 between 1966—70 and 1971—75. Because the sample of mountain women was small, any such apparent trends must be viewed with caution. It is more likely that fertility was relatively constant during the decade and a half prior to the survey. Terai women reported a rise in fertility at all ages between 1961—65 and 1966—70, part of which may have been genuine if it represented fertility recovery as malaria control was extended throughout the terai. Between 1966—70 and 1971—75, terai women reported no change in cumulative fertility up to age 35.

Therefore, in the three terrains of Nepal during 1961—75, there were steady fertility levels in all or almost all age groups of women, steady cumulative fertility up to age 35, and probably a steady total fertility rate. The one reported exception to this trend that might be

26 For a description of different patterns of fertility, see United Nations, ESA
    (1965:101—21).

genuine was a slight rise in fertility in the terai between 1961—65 and 1966—70, which could have resulted from malaria control. From these data we find no convincing evidence of a fertility decline in any age group in any terrain up to 1976.

The household and the individual level data from the NFS can be used to estimate Nepal's crude birth rate for the mid-1970s. In Table 15, we show the range of birth rates so derived. Three sets of age-specific fertility rates are used. The first is an adjusted fertility schedule from reported births during the 12 months prior to the survey, which was taken in mid-1976. The second consists of reported, unadjusted age-specific fertility rates for the 12 months preceding the NFS. The third is the fertility schedule averaged for the years 1971—75. Three age structures are used as well. The first column of Table 15 is based on the recorded age structure from the NFS household survey, the second on the same age structure smoothed to correct for age heaping, and the third on a model stable age structure appropriate for Nepal (see notes of Table 15).

TABLE 15 Estimates of crude birth rate (CBR) based on the 1976 Nepal Fertility Survey: Nepal, mid-1970s
(Rates per thousand population)

Age-specific fertility rate (ASFR) schedule	Female age structure		
	Recorded (unadjusted)	Corrected for age heaping[a]	Matched to a model stable population age structure[b]
1 Adjusted schedule based on births 12 months before survey	48.4	48.9	47.7
2 Fertility schedule (unadjusted) based on births 12 months before survey	48.7	47.0	45.8
3 Schedule based on average annual rates for 1971—75 period	46.3	46.8	45.6

a   Age structure corrected for age heaping is derived by applying Feeney (1979) method.

b   The age structure of level 11 of a West model stable population (Coale and Demeny, 1966: 94) with an implied total fertility rate of 6.3 and female life expectancy of about 44 years was selected as a reasonable alternative to the recorded age structure.

SOURCES for ASFR Schedule:
1   Goldman et al. (1979:21).
2   Calculated from the NFS individual and household data tapes.
3   Table 13.

Our crude birth rate estimates range from 45.6 to 48.9 per thousand population, slightly higher than most previous estimates for Nepal's birth rate in the mid-1970s. The Demographic Sample Surveys arrived at estimated crude birth rates of 44.7 for 1974–75, 46.8 for 1976, and 42.6 for 1977–78 after upward adjustments were made for underreporting (Bourini, 1976:14; Bourini, 1977:18). The U.S. Bureau of the Census estimated a 1974–76 crude birth rate of 45–47 for Nepal based on adjusted DSS data and a crude birth rate of 45 for 1976 based on unadjusted NFS data (United States, Bureau of the Census, 1978:198). More recently, another U.S. Census Bureau publication estimated a crude birth rate of 45 per thousand population for 1975, based on composite age-specific fertility rates from the Demographic Sample Surveys and the Nepal Fertility Survey, and on a 1975 age structure projected from the adjusted 1971 census age structure (Kramer, 1979:7). The absolute range of CBR difference in our estimates, as shown in Table 15, is three per thousand population. On the basis of these estimates, we conclude that as of the mid-1970s Nepal had a CBR of about 47 per thousand population.

To summarize, Nepal is still a high-fertility country. There is even evidence that Nepal's fertility since the early 1960s has been higher than it was before then. In particular, the terai may have experienced a rise in fertility in response to malaria control. Given the limitations of retrospective data, whether or not Nepal's fertility actually increased during the 1960s is not clear, but at least there is no indication of a continuing fertility increase after the late 1960s. Nepal's fertility during the early and mid-1970s was steady at about 6.1 to 6.3 births per woman, corresponding to a crude birth rate of about 47 per 1,000 population.

FAMILY PLANNING ATTITUDES AND PREVALENCE

Among the elite and the government leaders of Nepal, a recognition of the need for family planning came early in the development process. In 1958 a private family planning organization, the Nepal Family Planning Association, was formed in Kathmandu. Its members attempted to educate the public about family planning. Then in 1965, Nepal's government publicly acknowledged the need for a national family planning program. Nepal was one of only 12 countries to sign a United Nations Declaration of Population in 1966, which stated that family planning is a fundamental human right and an important element in long-range national planning (United Nations, 1967).

A clinic-based family planning program was established and expanded slowly in the Kathmandu Valley during the late 1960s. It emphasized the provision of intrauterine devices (IUDs), condoms, vasectomies, and oral contraceptives (David, 1969:11–16). But only after 1968 did family planning services begin to be provided outside the Kathmandu Valley. The program's emphasis during the 1968–74 period was on building family planning/maternal and child health (FP/MCH) clinics in scattered locations around the country, and on staffing them with paramedics and health workers with at least some training. Data reported by the clinics on acceptors of family planning services show that during the early 1970s condoms were chosen by 50–60 percent of acceptors and pills were chosen by 30–40 percent. Vasectomies accounted for only about 6 percent of acceptors by the mid-1970s though they accounted for greater proportions in earlier years (Pande, 1975:144). Most sterilizations have been provided by mobile camps. As of 1974, the number of IUD insertions and female sterilizations was negligible in the family planning program because many clinics were not equipped to provide these services or to offer immediate medical followup in case of complications.

NFS data can help us assess the effects of the family planning program nationwide as of 1976.[27] According to the survey results, only 3.7 percent of currently married women between the ages of 15 and 49 in 1976 had ever used any of the modern contraceptive methods offered by the program, and only 0.7 percent reported ever having used any folk method of contraception. Only 2.3 percent of currently married women were practicing any type of contraception at the time of the survey. These proportions are so small that Nepal can be described as almost a noncontracepting population as of the mid-1970s.

Of the tiny proportion of currently married women who were practicing contraception in 1976, 65 percent were protected from pregnancy by their husbands' vasectomies. Only 17 percent were protected by the pill, and 9 percent by condoms, whereas the proportions using other methods were small. More urban than rural women were using program methods, as would be expected. Sixteen percent of currently married urban women and 2 percent of currently married rural women were contracepting in 1976.[28] This difference may reflect a greater

27 Unless mentioned otherwise, the data reported here are computed from the 1976 Nepal Fertility Survey, individual data tape.

28 Because the urban population of Nepal constitutes only 4 percent of the total population, and the urban proportion of the NFS sample was accordingly small,

demand for contraception among more modern urban couples, the greater availability of most forms of contraception in urban areas, or both. Yet even among urban couples the level of birth control was very low in Nepal.

The 1965–66 Nepal Health Survey and the Nepal Fertility Survey of 1976 solicited information on ideal family size and attitude toward contraception. In general, when questioned in surveys about their "ideal" number of children, married women have reported average or modal answers clustering around four or five children.[29] In the Nepal Health Survey, 687 married women under age 50 answered the questions: "If you were just now getting married, how many boys would you like to have? how many girls?" (Worth and Shah, 1969:32–33), and their responses indicated a strong preference for sons. The average number of children wanted by respondents was 4.5. Respondents were also asked a more general question: "For a couple just getting married in this village, how many children would be ideal?" The average number was 5.0.

A decade later, the 1976 Nepal Fertility Survey asked a much larger and more representative sample of respondents: "If you could choose exactly the number of children to have in your whole life, how many children would that be?" The mean number of children wanted by the currently married women in the sample was 4.0 (Nepal, FP/MCH Project, 1977:158). Women over age 34 gave slightly higher numbers, averaging 4.3 children, whereas younger groups of women gave slightly lower numbers. For instance, women 15–24 years old wanted an average of 3.6 children.

In 1976 married women still desired to have four children on the average; and given the wording of the survey questions, respondents probably meant that they wanted an average of four children who would survive to adulthood. With high infant and child mortality levels in Nepal, women on average would require well over 4.0 births to achieve that goal. Nevertheless, there was a substantial proportion of

the sampling error for the urban sector was large. Of 124 currently married urban women in the sample, 20 were practicing contraception at the time of the survey. The figure of 16 percent should be considered only an approximation of urban contraceptive use in the country.

29 Survey questions on ideal family size often elicit unreliable responses because respondents are confused about the meaning of the questions and may answer differently depending on the exact wording. Therefore, the responses need to be assessed cautiously.

married women in Nepal who already had their desired number of
living children and were likely candidates for contraception. Westoff
(1978:15) has calculated from NFS interviews that, as of 1976, 21 percent of currently married women in Nepal were at risk of pregnancy
and wanted no more children, yet were not using any contraceptive
method. This is a measure of the "unmet need for contraception." It
is a conservative estimate because it assumes that couples need contraception only to cease childbearing and ignores the possible use of contraception for spacing births. There are various reasons why these
women, who appeared to need contraception, were not using it. Many
Nepalese women believe that the number of children they have is determined by fate, that they themselves have no control over their fertility, or should have no control over it. For example, currently married, fecund female respondents in the 1976 NFS who had never used
contraception (79 percent of all respondents) were asked: "Do you approve or disapprove of couples using a method to delay or avoid pregnancy?" and "Does your husband approve or disapprove of couples
using a method to delay or avoid pregnancy?" In reply to the first
question, 65 percent of the respondents said they disapproved of using
a contraceptive method, and only 29 percent approved. Similarly, in
response to the second question, although 39 percent of the women
said they did not know what their husbands thought, 43 percent said
that their husbands disapproved. Only 18 percent stated that their husbands approved.[30]

Another major impediment to the use of contraception is that respondents perceived contraceptive services to be inaccessible
(Rodríguez, 1979). Ninety-four percent of the NFS respondents said
they did not know where to go for family planning advice and supplies.[31] Of the 6 percent who said they knew where to go for contraception, many could not estimate distance or travel time to the family
planning outlet; and for those who ventured an estimate, the median
distance to the nearest contraceptive source was four miles and the
median time it would take to get there was two hours. Only 1 percent

---

30 Some of these negative responses may have reflected embarrassment at discussing matters relating to sexuality, or may mean that the questionnaire design
was problematic.

31 Some of the respondents may have misinterpreted the question that elicited
this response to have a more personal meaning, such as "Do you go there?"
The proportion not knowing where to get family planning services may thus
have been exaggerated (Campbell et al., 1979:52).

of currently married women reported ever having been to such a family planning outlet (Rodríguez, 1979:102).

The inaccessibility of birth control advice and supplies (as detected from responses to NFS questions) helps to explain the low level of contraceptive use in Nepal, independent of the other factors that might be expected to influence contraceptive use (Rodríguez, 1979: 113—15). Therefore, a top priority in Nepal's family planning program should be to make birth control methods available to remote households and villages on a regular basis with adequate followup.

It would, however, be incorrect to assume that once program methods are available and accessible, most eligible couples will start contracepting to prevent or terminate childbearing, or to space births. Some couples can be expected to do so, but they might not represent any sizable proportion of eligible couples. The NFS data presented in Table 16 help us assess some of the likely future prospects for contraceptive use. The data show that of all ever married Nepalese women surveyed, only about 8 percent intended to use a contraceptive method in the future (column 1), whereas 71 percent had not used and did not intend to (column 2).[32] Of the women in age groups 25—29 and 30—34, over three-fourths did not intend to use contraception, and only about 11 percent indicated their intention to use it. Only about 2 percent of all of the ever married women had used a method in the past during a birth interval (columns 4—6). If these data are any indication of the future contraceptive pattern in Nepal, users (including former users) will represent only about 10 percent of ever married women in the near future. Interestingly, 10 percent is only about half of the proportion of women who had heard of at least one efficient family planning method (Nepal, FP/MCH Project, 1977: 63, table 7.2). If 10 percent of ever married women used contraception, this would represent over four times the proportion who were contracepting in 1976, but the level of overall usage would still not be high. Family planning motivational work would be needed in order to expand contraceptive use further.

Methods offered by Nepal's family planning program do not include abortion, because abortion is illegal except to save the life of a pregnant woman. Almost none of Nepal's overwhelmingly rural population has access to safe abortions. This situation forces most Nepalese

32 It should, however, be mentioned that this figure also includes some women who were undecided about using contraception (see note in Table 16).

TABLE 16 Percentage distribution of all ever married women according to pattern of contraceptive use by current age: Nepal, 1976

Age group	Pattern of contraceptive use.									Total %	Total number
	Never used but intend to (1)	Never used and do not intend to (2)	Never used and now no need (3)	Used in open interval (4)	Used in last closed interval (5)	Used in some earlier interval (6)	Sterilized (7)	Current user (8)	Used but no longer fecund (9)		
15–19	6.7	88.5	3.6	.3	.1	.4	.0	.3	.0	100.0	741
20–24	8.6	86.5	2.6	.5	.4	.3	.3	.7	.0	100.0	1,226
25–29	11.5	79.9	3.7	.5	.7	1.4	1.5	.6	.2	100.0	1,146
30–34	9.9	74.5	9.2	.6	.9	.5	2.9	1.3	.1	100.0	855
35–39	8.2	66.0	18.8	.5	1.1	.8	3.1	1.1	.4	100.0	736
40–44	4.3	47.1	44.0	.4	.4	.8	1.7	.3	1.0	100.0	720
45–49	.6	23.3	73.4	.4	.2	.4	1.2	.2	.4	100.0	516
All women	7.9	70.9	17.1	.5	.6	.7	1.5	.7	.3	100.0	5,940

NOTES: In the construction of "pattern of contraceptive use," all respondents were classified into three major groups of (1) never users, (2) past but not current users, and (3) current users.

(1) Never users were then divided into three subcategories: intend to use in the future; do not intend to (or undecided about) use in the future; and those who at the time of the survey were infecund or no longer married (i.e., had no need for contraception) and who were therefore not asked the question on future intentions.

(2) Past users were divided into four subcategories according to recency of use: in the open birth interval, in the last closed birth interval, in some earlier interval; the fourth group comprises respondents who were no longer fecund.

(3) Current users were divided into two subcategories according to whether they had been sterilized for contraceptive purposes or were currently using some other method.

SOURCE: Based on Nepal, FP/MCH Project (1977:224, table 4.5.1).

women to carry unwanted or high-risk pregnancies to term or to resort to unsafe abortions that may jeopardize their lives. In recent years, however, some leading groups in Kathmandu have discussed the legalization of abortion. A governmental Task Force on Population Policy recommended in 1974:

Liberal policy should be followed on the legalization of abortion. . . . If an abortion is performed on the joint written application of the couple, legal provision should be made so that no punishment is made on doctors, nurses, concerned personnel and accessories. On the other hand, abortion either by medicine or by surgical means by persons without any training should be made strictly punishable (Nepal, National Planning Commission Secretariat, 1974a:37).

Participants in a Conference on the Implementation of Population Policies, held in Kathmandu in 1976, were more divided in their approach to abortion. A report on general discussion from the floor stated:

Many abortions are carried out illegally; hence, the law should be modified, if not liberalized, to allow this to be done safely. However, there was some controversy over this issue. The consensus was that abortion should be used only as a last resort for couples (Nepal, Population Policies Coordination Board, 1976:160).

But a working group of the conference who concentrated on policies needed for expanding the roles of women and reducing their fertility recommended that abortion be legalized (p. 167).

The NFS included a series of attitudinal questions on abortion, but unfortunately the sequence of questions may have been inappropriate for Nepal. Ninety-five percent of the ever married female respondents answered the first abortion question ("Have you ever heard of abortion?") by saying they had not; those women were not asked any of the attitudinal questions. Of the 5 percent who were asked about their attitudes toward abortion, most approved of abortion if pregnancy is dangerous to the woman's health, approximately half approved of abortion for unmarried women and half disapproved, and most disapproved of abortion as a backup for contraceptive failure or as an option for people who cannot afford or do not want more children. It is somewhat startling that so many women stated they had never heard of abortion. It may be that many had genuinely never heard of this procedure. There may also have been a problem in the way the question was phrased; and it is possible that because abortion is not considered a proper topic for open discussion in Nepalese society, respondents feigned ignorance of the procedure.[33] We must await future research for more probing on this topic.

To summarize, it has been over a decade since Nepal's family planning program was officially launched. The emphasis during most of this period has been on setting up a family planning supply infrastructure, with at least one clinic in each district of the country. As of 1976, only a tiny proportion of married couples were using birth control measures. The desired number of children per woman was still high (around four). There was a significant unmet need for birth control as of 1976; one-quarter of currently married women interviewed in the Nepal Fertility Survey stated that they wanted no more children, yet very few of them were doing anything to prevent another pregnancy. Data suggest that inaccessibility of family planning services and supplies was partly responsible for nonuse of modern methods. It appears, however, that ready availability of birth control techniques will not automatically lead to a high level contraceptive use in the near future in Nepal.

MIGRATION AND URBANIZATION

Migration

Because almost all Nepalese live and work in the agricultural sector, migration patterns of Nepal are closely connected to the availability of usable agricultural land. During the eighteenth and nineteenth centuries, Nepal had low population density, a chronic shortage of adult workers in agriculture and for military purposes, and an abundance of area available for cultivation (Regmi, 1971:78–102). After the political unification of Nepal in the 1790s, the government encouraged Tibetans to immigrate to the Himalayan northern strip of Nepal and Indians to immigrate to the terai and inner terai areas. The apparent purpose of this government policy was to increase population density, agricultural production, and government revenue from agricultural taxes, particularly along the extended southern and northern borders of the country. In general, the policy was successful in attracting

---

33 Because of the sensitivity of this topic, respondents may have interpreted the first question to have a more threatening meaning than intended, so that a negative answer meant "No, I haven't had an abortion" or "No, I am not familiar with abortion technique" (Campbell et al., 1979:49–52).

immigrants, but an increasing concentration of land ownership and almost intolerable oppression of peasants in hill and terai areas caused counterstreams of emigration to India during the nineteenth century (Regmi, 1971:143–47, 179–86, 192–95). In addition, the British East India Company began recruiting Nepalese mercenaries after 1816. Though historical migration data are scarce, it appears that net migration flows in the early nineteenth century were from India to a narrow southern strip of the terai, from Tibet to the mountains of Nepal, and from the hills of Nepal to India (Regmi, 1971:196–97). The emigration from the hills may have resulted from growing scarcity of agricultural land in the hill areas, increasing concentration of land ownership, and better economic opportunities in India.

These same migration flows increased in intensity during the Rana period, 1846–1950. The government encouraged Indians to settle on that strip of the terai closest to the Indian border, with some success. Government policy also encouraged the opening up of the densely forested northern edges of the terai by settlers from Nepal's hills. This settlement was slow and halting, hampered by the deadly malarial climate of the terai and inner terai.

Meanwhile, natural population increase in the hill areas was putting increasing pressure on the arable land there. (See section on population growth and agricultural production.) Agricultural techniques remained in a primitive state and continued to produce low yields. Surplus population had to relocate elsewhere, but Nepal's hill people were generally unwilling to risk the danger and discomfort of the hot and malarial terai, where there was ample unused land. Rather, after 1850 many hill people moved from Nepal eastward to Assam, Darjeeling, Sikkim, Burma, and Bhutan. They were attracted in part by free plots of land given to plantation workers in Darjeeling and Assam, and by the availability of land in Bhutan and Sikkim. There is also evidence that "a sizable number of the emigrants consisted of slaves and debtors who were harassed by their owners and creditors, [who] expropriated their lands" (Regmi, 1978:134). The development of coal and tea industries in different areas of India created job markets for unskilled labor from Nepal during the late nineteenth century (Regmi, 1978:134–35). Another major migration flow from the hills of Nepal during the twentieth century has been the temporary movement of adult males looking for employment as Gurkha soldiers in British and Indian armies.

Most of the recent data on migration come from the censuses of 1952/54, 1961, and 1971. The data are not strictly comparable and are inadequate for a detailed analysis of Nepal's migration patterns, but they furnish a general picture of the movement of the people within and outside Nepal.

In the 1952/54 census, which was a *de jure* count, only persons who had been absent from home six months or more were recorded as migrants. The procedure underestimated the amount of migration that had occurred prior to the census because persons who had moved away permanently but had been gone less than six months were counted at their previous homes, not at their new locations, and whole families who had moved were counted in their new locations if still living in Nepal, rather than recorded as migrants, or not counted at all if they had emigrated from Nepal.

The 1952/54 census indicated that 216,853 persons, or 2.6 percent of the enumerated population, had been absent from home six months or more (Nepal, Department of Statistics, 1958:50—51). Ninety-seven percent of all such migrants were from the hills and mountains, and almost none from the terai and inner terai. Eighty-seven percent of the migrants were male, almost all of whom were in the age range of 15—44. Most (91 percent) of the people recorded as migrants were living abroad, and of those nearly all were in India. Of the 9 percent (or 18,733) who were residing elsewhere in Nepal, 41 percent had gone to Kathmandu Valley, 19 percent had gone to the eastern terai, and 8 percent had gone to other parts of the terai. The rest had moved to the inner terai (this was before malaria control work had begun) and to other parts of the hills. From the limited data available, it appears that Nepal's population was still relatively immobile in the early 1950s, that there was little internal migration, and that almost all the emigration was by males who moved from the hills and mountains of Nepal to India. Unfortunately, these data do not capture whole-family migration or immigration into Nepal before 1952/54.

The 1961 census, which was also a *de jure* count, elicited information on persons who were away from home six months or more, plus information on the foreign-born residing in Nepal and on the place of birth of respondents. These data can help us detect some long-term migration trends. As of 1961, 4.0 percent of the counted population (or 386,824 persons) had been away from home six months or more (Nepal, CEDA, 1973:16). This figure suggests that migration of

individual family members had increased substantially between 1952/
54 and 1961. As was the case in 1952/54, almost all these 1961 migrants had moved from the hills and mountains of Nepal. Of those
absent from home, 85 percent were abroad (Nepal, CBS, 1977:12),
and for over 90 percent of the emigrants the country of destination
was India (Tuladhar et al., 1978:42). In India, the most common
destinations of the Nepalese migrants were Assam, Bihar, Uttar
Pradesh, and West Bengal. Migrants living abroad increased from 2.3
percent of the total counted population in 1952/54 to 3.4 percent in
1961; migrants living elsewhere in Nepal increased from 0.2 percent
to 0.6 percent.[34] Further details are not available on the sex ratios or
the destinations of these migrants. There are no comparable data on
persons away from home six months or more in the 1971 census, because in 1971 anyone away from home six months or more was
counted in the new location in Nepal, and family members who were
abroad were not counted at all.

The 1961 and 1971 censuses asked all respondents about their place
of birth. From this information, it is possible to compare where someone was born with where he or she was living at census time. There
are problems with using this information as a measure of migration,
because persons might have made any number of moves after leaving
their place of birth and before arriving at their current location, and
migrants who previously left their birthplace but later returned and
were there at census time are lost from this measure of migration; but
at least it detects persons who were no longer living at their birthplace
and had migrated at least once. Tables 17 and 18 present census data
on lifetime internal migration—that is, migration of persons who had
moved from their birthplace in Nepal at least six months prior to census time to another location in Nepal. Unfortunately, the two tables
are not strictly comparable because different regional and terrain
boundaries were used for the two censuses.

Despite these limitations, some interesting conclusions can be
drawn from these tables concerning the pattern of internal migration.
In 1961, the number of persons who had moved from their area of

---

34 In 1952/54, 198,120 persons were living abroad and 18,733 persons were living
   elsewhere within Nepal out of 8,473,478 persons counted (Nepal, Department
   of Statistics, 1958:50). In 1961, 328,470 persons were abroad and 58,354 persons were elsewhere in Nepal out of a total counted population of 9,794,820
   (Nepal, CEDA, 1973:16; Nepal, CBS, 1977:12).

TABLE 17 Lifetime internal migration: Nepal, 1961

Area	Lifetime in-migrants	Lifetime out-migrants	Net lifetime migration
Eastern hills and mountains	5,354	74,846	−69,492
Eastern inner terai	5,345	10,552	−5,207
Eastern terai	72,030	3,848	+68,182
Western and central hills and mountains	5,694	38,326	−32,632
Kathmandu Valley	24,748	20,131	+4,617
Western inner terai	3,446	16,754	−13,308
Central inner terai	27,560	2,188	+25,372
Western and central terai	8,307	2,591	+5,716
Far western hills and mountains	4,783	8,656	−3,873
Far western terai	21,170	545	+20,625
All areas	178,437	178,437	0

NOTE: This table compares current district of residence with reported district of birth only for respondents present at home for the census or gone less than six months. It excludes persons absent from home at census time. It also excludes migrants to or from foreign countries and persons whose place of birth was unstated. In the 1961 census, data for the terai were subdivided into inner terai and terai.

SOURCE: Nepal, CBS (1967: vol. 2, table 11).

birth was still relatively small, comprising only 1.9 percent of the 9,412,996 persons who were at home for the census.[35] By 1971 the number of such lifetime internal migrants had increased to 4.4 percent of those present at home for the census. Nepal still had a relatively immobile population, but during 1961−71 there had been a notable increase in internal migration.

Before 1961, districts that had lost the largest number of persons to other areas of Nepal were in the eastern, central, and western hills and the mountains. The western inner terai had also lost population. The districts that had gained the greatest influx of internal migrants were the eastern terai, central inner terai, and far western terai. Already the movement of migrants from Nepal's hills and mountains to the terai had become a detectable pattern. No longer were internal migrants

35 Even if all 58,354 persons counted as absent from their home for more than six months but present in Nepal in 1961 are designated as lifetime migrants to make 1961 census data more comparable with 1971 data, this increases the total of lifetime internal migrants to only 2.5 percent of the population present at home for the 1961 census.

TABLE 18 Lifetime internal migration: Nepal, 1971

Area	Lifetime in-migrants	Lifetime out-migrants	Net lifetime migration
Eastern mountains	6,385	37,916	−31,531
Eastern hills	17,498	186,843	−169,345
Eastern terai	185,799	10,267	+175,532
Kathmandu Valley	26,440	45,484	−19,044
Central mountains	1,223	2,095	−872
Central hills	29,752	140,642	−110,890
Central terai	161,751	6,504	+155,247
Western mountains	2,125	9,681	−7,556
Western hills	5,063	65,750	−60,687
Western terai	70,885	1,739	+69,146
All areas	506,921	506,921	0

NOTE: This table compares current district of residence with reported district of birth only for respondents present at home for the census or gone less than six months. It excludes migrants to or from foreign countries. In the 1971 census, "terai" includes inner terai as well.

SOURCE: Nepal, CBS (1975a: vol. 2, prt. 1, table 10).

moving primarily to the Kathmandu Valley; by 1961 the number of lifetime out-migrants from the Kathmandu Valley had almost caught up with the number of lifetime in-migrants.

Map 3 and Table 19 provide a closer look at lifetime internal migration between districts and regions as of the 1971 census. Nearly 65 percent of Nepal's internal migrants originated from the eastern and central hills. The vast majority of migrants from the eastern hills, 149,401 out of 186,843, moved to the eastern terai and inner terai areas. Almost all of the migrants from the central hills, 123,378 out of 140,642, migrated to the central terai. The western hills also lost population, almost completely to the western terai. Lifetime internal migration from Nepal's hill areas consisted almost totally of north-to-south migration streams to adjacent sections of the terai.

Migrants from the mountains, however, moved primarily to the terai of the same region, rather than to the hills, even though the hills are closer to their point of origin. From the eastern mountains, 56 percent of out-migrants moved to the eastern terai, whereas 22 percent migrated to the eastern hills. Similarly, 60 percent of lifetime migrants

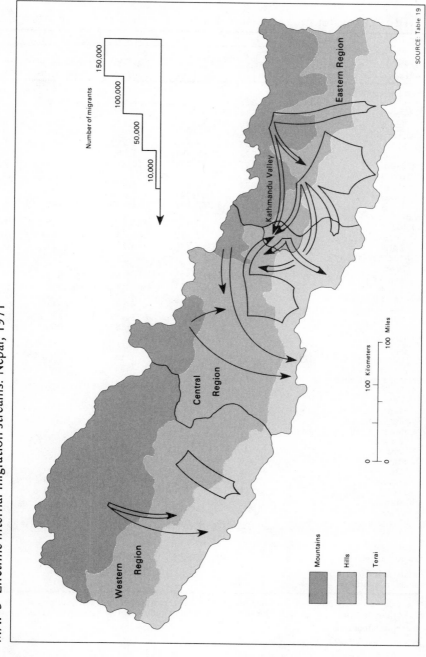

MAP 3 Lifetime internal migration streams: Nepal, 1971

Number of migrants

150,000

100,000

50,000

10,000

Eastern Region

Kathmandu Valley

Central Region

Western Region

Mountains

Hills

Terai

100 Kilometers

100 Miles

0

0

SOURCE Table 19

73

TABLE 19 Lifetime internal migration of native-born population, by

Origin and sex	Destination					
	Eastern mountains	Eastern hills	Eastern terai	Kathmandu Valley	Central mountains	Central hills
Eastern mountains						
Male	316,103	1,856	11,369	1,885	6	718
Female	316,726	6,534	9,846	1,600	3	632
Total	632,829	8,390	21,215	3,485	9	1,350
Eastern hills						
Male	1,481	809,563	79,750	5,152	44	4,201
Female	3,573	825,778	69,651	5,064	20	3,735
Total	5,054	1,635,341	149,401	10,216	64	7,936
Eastern terai						
Male	194	1,811	977,749	1,059	5	202
Female	165	1,930	886,223	649	0	166
Total	359	3,741	1,863,972	1,708	5	368
Kathmandu Valley						
Male	412	1,781	4,943	300,805	108	7,796
Female	270	3,087	3,783	285,346	14	7,376
Total	682	4,868	8,726	586,151	122	15,172
Central mountains						
Male	0	2	36	74	24,910	236
Female	0	9	25	67	24,459	366
Total	0	11	61	141	49,369	602
Central hills						
Male	124	103	1,643	5,338	415	1,156,299
Female	101	243	929	3,343	585	1,193,534
Total	225	346	2,572	8,681	1,000	2,349,833
Central terai						
Male	17	46	1,302	660	5	717
Female	12	65	2,097	481	5	709
Total	29	111	3,399	1,141	10	1,426
Western mountains						
Male	4	2	23	92	2	33
Female	1	2	10	44	11	79
Total	5	4	33	136	13	112
Western hills						
Male	18	4	142	437	0	559
Female	12	15	100	179	0	2,151
Total	30	19	242	616	0	2,710
Western terai						
Male	1	6	70	201	0	45
Female	0	2	80	115	0	31
Total	1	8	150	316	0	76
All origins						
Male	2,251	5,611	99,278	14,898	585	14,507
Female	4,134	11,887	86,521	11,542	638	15,245
Total	6,385	17,498	185,799	26,440	1,223	29,752
% of total in-migrants	1.3	3.5	36.7	5.2	0.2	5.9
Males per 100 female in-migrants	54.5	47.2	114.7	129.1	91.7	95.2

NOTE: Table excludes foreign-born persons (2.9 percent of the total population) and Nepal-
  origin and destination were the same, shown diagonally from the top left to the bottom

nc—not calculated.

na—not applicable.

SOURCE: Nepal, CBS (1975a: vol. 2, prt. 1, table 10).

sex: Nepal, 1971

Central terai	Western mountains	Western hills	Western terai	Total out-migrants	% of total out-migrants	Males per 100 female out-migrants
1,809	6	4	74	17,727	nc	na
1,544	1	3	26	20,189	nc	na
3,353	7	7	100	37,916	7.5	87.8
7,200	7	34	587	98,456	nc	na
6,109	2	18	215	88,387	nc	na
13,309	9	52	802	186,843	36.9	111.4
1,492	11	28	173	4,975	nc	na
2,237	6	13	126	5,292	nc	na
3,729	17	41	299	10,267	2.0	94.0
6,610	33	643	1,307	23,633	nc	na
5,763	20	707	831	21,851	nc	na
12,373	53	1,350	2,138	45,484	9.0	108.2
694	0	1	11	1,054	nc	na
568	1	0	5	1,041	nc	na
1,262	1	1	16	2,095	0.4	101.2
64,879	62	331	1,797	74,692	nc	na
58,499	29	1,090	1,131	65,950	nc	na
123,378	91	1,421	2,928	140,642	27.7	113.2
667,020	8	30	177	2,962	nc	na
578,664	3	20	150	3,542	nc	na
1,245,684	11	50	327	6,504	1.3	83.6
33	225,136	387	4,303	4,879	nc	na
31	217,604	1,041	3,583	4,802	nc	na
64	442,740	1,428	7,886	9,681	1.9	101.6
2,065	347	691,610	29,461	33,033	nc	na
1,751	1,581	709,774	26,928	32,717	nc	na
3,816	1,928	1,401,384	56,389	65,750	13.0	101.0
230	5	214	262,345	772	nc	na
237	3	499	241,966	967	nc	na
467	8	713	504,311	1,739	0.3	79.8
85,012	479	1,672	37,890	262,183	51.7	na
76,739	1,646	3,391	32,995	244,738	48.3	na
161,751	2,125	5,063	70,885	506,921	100.0	107.1
31.9	0.4	1.0	14.0	100.1	na	na
110.8	29.1	49.3	114.8	107.1	na	na

ese who had been abroad for more than six months. Lifetime nonmigrants (i.e., those whose
right of the table) are excluded from calculations of in- and out-migration and of sex ratios.

from the central mountains moved to the central terai, and 29 percent to the central hills. The same pattern emerged for the western mountains; 81 percent of the migrants moved to the western terai, whereas 15 percent moved to the western hills. From the mountains and hills, most internal migration was from north to south toward a lower altitude. The only significant lateral movements were from one terai area to another or into and out of Kathmandu Valley. It is noteworthy that between 1961 and 1971, Kathmandu Valley no longer drew many Nepal-born lifetime in-migrants, but rather lost a sizable number of people to out-migration. According to the 1971 census, 45,484 persons had left Kathmandu Valley for other areas of Nepal, while only 26,440 persons born elsewhere in Nepal had migrated to Kathmandu Valley. As of 1971, therefore, Kathmandu Valley had not experienced the rapid growth through internal migration that has characterized the metropolitan areas of many developing countries.

Both "pull" and "push" factors have led to the increasing migration streams (as detected from the census data) from the mountains and hills to the terai. One major factor leading people to be pushed out of the mountains and hills is the unavailability of usable land for cultivation, coupled with population pressure and declining agricultural productivity. In addition, the decreasing role of the trans-Himalayan trade (trade between Nepal and Tibet has been restricted since the late 1950s) may also have aggravated the economic situation of the mountains and some of the upper hill areas, thus forcing people to move elsewhere. On the "pull" side, a major factor for migration to the terai has been the opening up of new agricultural land following malaria control. The terai became a new "promised land" for the people in the hills and mountains. The colonization of the terai by the hill and mountain people has resulted in spontaneous as well as planned settlements.

Among lifetime internal migrants, males moved more than females (Table 19). About 107 males moved from their birthplace for every 100 females. In particular, a predominance of males migrated from hill areas and from Kathmandu Valley. Similarly, among migrants from within Nepal to the terai, 115 males for every 100 females moved into the eastern and western terai, and 111 males per 100 females migrated into the central terai. Kathmandu Valley in particular attracted more male lifetime in-migrants than female—129 males for every 100 females.

. The question on place of birth in the 1961 and 1971 censuses also elicited information on lifetime immigration from abroad. In the 1961 census, 337,620 persons, or 3.6 percent of the counted population, said they were born outside of Nepal. In 1971, 337,448 persons, or 2.9 percent of the counted population, said they were born abroad (Tuladhar et al., 1978:40). These data suggest that during the 1960s Nepal received only enough immigrants to replace those lost through death and emigration, and may indicate that rates of immigration declined from earlier levels, though we have no annual immigration data with which to test this.

Why were there so few immigrants during 1961–71? According to both censuses, 96 percent of the foreign-born in Nepal came from India, and almost all of the India-born immigrants had moved to the terai. Something prevented any sizable immigration from India to the Nepal terai during the decade. It was not border checkpoints, because there is an open border between Nepal and India in the terai. The probable cause was Nepal government policy, which then, as now, attempted to discourage further Indian immigration into the terai while encouraging the "Nepalization" of the terai and inner terai through internal migration from the hills (Gaige, 1975). Gaige (1975:81–83, 91–107) has reported that the government gives most of the terai land confiscated from tribal people through the land reform program which began in the early 1960s to settlers from the hills and that it systematically settles retired Gurkha soldiers (who are mostly hill people) in the terai. Most important, the Nepal Constitution of 1962 made it difficult for Indian immigrants to the terai to acquire Nepalese citizenship; and the government began requiring Nepalese citizenship for ownership of small firms, preferential hiring in industries and teaching jobs, and especially the ownership of land. These latter restrictions have probably made immigration less attractive to Indians than before.

The government's policy of Nepalizing the terai seems to have met with success. As of 1961, 11 percent of the terai population was foreign-born (and nearly all the foreign born were from India), only 3 percent was born in the hills and mountains of Nepal, and the vast majority of the terai population was born in the terai. By 1971, only 8 percent of the terai population was from India, whereas over 10 percent was from Nepal's hills and mountains (Rana and Thapa, 1975:44). The influx of settlers into the terai from higher altitudes in Nepal far exceeded immigration from India during the 1960s. Nevertheless, the population of the terai continues to consist mostly of persons who were born there, the majority of whom are culturally and linguistically linked to India's northern states because of the historical immigration pattern. A likely prospect for the next few decades is that the long-settled southern strip of the terai will continue to be inhabited predominantly by terai-born people, whereas the parts of the terai that were heavily forested until the 1960s may become dominated by people from the hills and mountains of Nepal.[36] These previously forested areas now being settled by hill people include the northern half of the eastern, central, and western terai, almost the whole far western terai, and all the inner terai areas.

We have seen that there was little immigration to Nepal during 1961—71. What about emigration from Nepal? Unfortunately, recent data on this movement are seriously deficient. We know that there was an increase in the proportion of Nepal's population recorded in the 1961 census as absent from home and out of the country compared with 1952/54, and that over 90 percent of such emigrants were in India. The censuses of India have recorded the number of persons born in Nepal who were residing in India, and the number increased greatly during the 1950s, from 279,000 in 1951 to 493,400 in 1961 (Rana and Thapa, 1975:67; India, Office of the Registrar General, 1971:8). The increase suggests rapid net migration flow to India in that decade. The 1971 Census of India counted 486,600 Nepal-born persons in India (India, Office of the Registrar General, 1971:8), a slight decline from the 1961 figure, which indicates a sharp decline in the net flow of Nepal-born migrants to India between the 1950s and the 1960s. The main reason why the long-term migration of Nepal-born persons to India became less pronounced in the 1960s is that the destination of many migrants leaving the hills of Nepal shifted from India to the Nepal terai (Table 19). This change was due primarily to malaria control and the sudden availability of good agricultural land in the terai. Shifts in the relative value of Indian and Nepalese currencies in the late 1960s also made it less attractive for migrants from the hills to go work in India.

Weiner (1973:620—24) has investigated the pattern of emigration from Nepal to India using 1961 Indian census data. Though useful, his analysis explores Nepal's emigration patterns only prior to the last

36 Gaige (1975:69) presents a map depicting settlement patterns in the terai forested areas as of 1967, and discusses future terai settlement prospects (pp. 85—86).

two decades. The 1961 Indian census asked where people were born, how long they had resided in India, and whether they were in the labor force. Most Nepal-born persons living in India in 1961 were residing in the northern and northeastern states of India, particularly in Uttar Pradesh, Bihar, West Bengal, and Assam. Most came from the Nepal hills.

Of the 493,400 Nepal-born persons counted, 277,200 were males and 216,200 were females (India, Office of the Registrar General, 1971:8). Though the numbers of males and females were similar, the pattern of migration was quite different for the two sexes. Of the 82,000 Nepal-born persons who had resided in India less than one year, 66,000 were males and only 16,000 were females. Many more males than females came from Nepal to India each year, but the males tended to leave within five years whereas the females tended to remain. Eighty-three percent of the Nepal-born males in India were employed in 1961, compared with 36 percent of the Nepal-born females. It appears that, as of 1961, Nepalese men went to India to work for a year or longer, then returned to Nepal, whereas Nepalese women followed their husbands to India, went to India to marry and settle down there, or in a minority of cases went to India for a short while to work. Weiner (1973:621) concluded:

... approximately 82,000 Nepalis migrated annually to India as of the 1961 census, and each year approximately 62,000 migrants returned after having lived in India from one to five years. Of the 20,000 who remained, half were males and half were females and at least half of these females came to India to marry Indian citizens.

The movement of women across the Nepal-India border for the purpose of marriage has not been a one-way phenomenon. In 1961 the sex ratio of the foreign-born in Nepal was only 56 (56 male for each 100 female immigrants), and in 1971 only 58 (Tuladhar et al., 1978: 41). One reason for the low sex ratio of foreign-born persons in Nepal could be that many women from India move into the nearby Nepal terai to marry and settle down. Citizenship restrictions in Nepal are not a serious problem for these women, because women who marry Nepal citizens automatically become citizens themselves.

It is difficult to trace changes in the patterns of migration flow from Nepal to India since 1961. Most of the relevant data from the 1971 Census of India are not yet published. We do know that the number of Nepal-born females counted in the Indian censuses increased from

216,200 in 1961 to 239,600 in 1971 (India, Office of Registrar General, 1971:8). This small increase probably means that the movement of Nepal-born women to India for marriage continued during the 1960s, although at a slower rate than in the 1950s. In both censuses, the great majority of Nepal-born women were reported to be living in rural areas—about 85 percent in 1961 and 1971. In contrast to the female pattern, the total number of Nepal-born males in India dropped from 277,200 in 1961 to 247,000 in 1971. Many of the men from the Nepal hills who under former conditions would have gone to India to work probably went to the Nepal terai during the 1960s instead. The proportion of Nepal-born males in rural areas of India stayed about the same—about 63 percent in 1961 and 1971.

Emigration to India from the hills of Nepal has served to relieve some of the population pressure in the hills while bringing in income for hill families. Nepalese workers in India send home or bring remittances when they return to Nepal. In addition, retired Gurkha soldiers who have returned to Nepal receive pensions from the Indian or British governments.

For Nepal, therefore, permanent migration serves to redistribute population from the hard-pressed hill and mountain areas to the relatively sparsely populated terai or to India, and temporary or seasonal migration abroad or elsewhere in Nepal enables workers to supplement the incomes of their hill families, who otherwise might not be able to remain in the hills. During the winter, the agricultural and herding families in Nepal's hills and mountains have little productive work to do there. Large-scale migration (so far undocumented in number) takes place every year, in which individuals or families move southward to lower altitudes, often accompanied by their animals. The purpose of this seasonal migration is, for some migrants, to graze the family animals through the winter and, for others, to earn sustenance or extra income from trading and other odd jobs, including harvesting or planting work in the terai where the agricultural season is longer than in the hills or mountains. All these forms of migration are partial solutions to the growing imbalance between the needs of an increasing population in the hills and the low level of per capita income that can currently be produced in the hills.

Some of the causes of hill-to-terai migration have been documented by a small sample survey of 435 permanent migrant households conducted in a section of the far western terai around 1975 (Nepal,

CEDA, 1977).[37] Eighty-three percent of the household heads had
been farmers in the hills; the rest had been wage earners or self-
employed in small business. At their terai destination, 95 percent of
the respondents were farmers. On one hand, the migrant families had
access to much more land in the terai than they had had in the hills.
Whereas 36 percent of the households had less than 1 *bigha* (1 bigha =
0.68 hectare) of land in the hills for example, only 6 percent of the
households had the use of less than 1 bigha of land at the terai destination. The proportion of respondent households tilling 1−11 bighas of
land increased from 44 percent in the hills to 87 percent in the terai.
On the other hand, though the migrant families were able to increase
their access to cultivated land by moving to the terai, some were
forced to shift from the status of landowner to tenant in the process.
A majority of the surveyed families owned their land at both origin
and destination, but the proportion who were tenants increased from
14 percent at origin to 30 percent at destination.

When asked why they had left the hills and moved to the terai, the
majority of households interviewed cited population pressures, increasing family size, and declining production from their farms as major
reasons (Nepal, CEDA, 1977:88−90). Many respondents also cited environmental deterioration such as flooding and landslides as a reason
for their move. Thus "push" factors appeared to be the primary motivations for moving from the hills. Some "pull" factors were also cited
by the migrants. A third of respondents said that a reason for the
move was that land was available in the terai for settlement. Others
said they had moved to the terai in part because they had heard that
terai land was relatively cheap or because they thought there were employment opportunities in the terai.

Thus, if respondents to this survey were characteristic of others who
have moved from the hills to the terai, the primary motivations for mi-
grating are population pressure on available resources, ecological deterioration of farmlands, and marginal economic status at point of
origin. Most of the surveyed families appear to have had little choice
but to move. Though push factors were predominant, pull factors
were also a consideration in drawing migrant families to the terai.

According to a recent survey referring to migration during a one-

37 This study also dealt with the causes of seasonal migration in the far western region. Another survey, by Toffin (1976), studied seasonal and permanent migration from a valley in the central hills, and came to similar conclusions.

year period in 1976—77 (Nepal, National Planning Commission Secretariat, 1978:82—83), 5.4 percent of the mountain population, 6.4
percent of the hill population, and 1.5 percent of the terai population
migrated during that year. This information indicates that hill and
mountain populations are relatively more mobile than the population
of the terai. The figures include seasonal and short-term migrants as
well as those who left home in 1976—77 for longer stays, but they
probably exclude the migration of whole households abroad. Sixty-
eight percent of the migrants reported by the surveyed households
left the country, 16 percent migrated to the terai or within the terai,
14 percent migrated to the hills or within the hills, and 1 percent migrated to the mountains or within the mountains.

Migration patterns noted from these data are, however, not directly
comparable with the lifetime migration data from the censuses. The
survey may have largely reflected the frequency of temporary migration, which is not available from the censuses of Nepal. These survey
data clearly suggest that migration abroad was a major phenomenon in
the country as of the mid-1970s.

The 1976—77 survey also reveals migration patterns by terrain.
Among mountain people, 83 percent of the migrants had left Nepal,
14 percent had gone to the hills of Nepal, and 3 percent had moved
within the mountains. It is striking that no surveyed households reported migration from the mountains to the terai, especially con-
sidering the strong lifetime internal migration stream from mountains
to terai prior to 1971. This unexpected result may mean that migrants
from the mountains changed their destinations from the terai in the
1960s to other areas in the 1970s, or it may reflect an error in the
survey design that caused mountain-to-terai migration to be missed.
Among hill people, 71 percent of the migrants went out of the country, 15 percent moved within the hills, 13 percent went to the terai,
and only 1 percent went to the mountains. These data indicate that,
although some movement from the hills to terai continued as in the
1960s, the primary destination of hill migrants in 1976—77 was
abroad and there was considerable lateral movement within the hills.
Lateral movement was most pronounced in the terai, as lifetime migration data from the 1971 census also indicated. Forty-nine percent
of terai migrants had moved within the terai, 34 percent had gone
abroad, 11 percent had moved to the hills, and 6 percent had moved
to the mountains.

Urbanization

A striking feature of Nepal's migration pattern in recent decades is that, in contrast to most other developing countries, Nepal seems to be experiencing little rural-to-urban migration. The three most recent censuses have recorded the urban population. A "nagar panchayat" (urban area) is defined as consisting of 5,000 or more inhabitants and such facilities as administrative offices, mills and factories, market and trade centers, transportation and communication, water supplies, and electricity. The 1952/54 census listed ten areas as urban, and their populations comprised 2.8 percent of the total population of that census. The urban population in the 1961 and 1971 censuses represented 3.6 and 4.0 percent of the total population, respectively. The data suggest that the level of urbanization in Nepal has remained very low. Both the 1961 and the 1971 censuses reported 16 urban areas, although some of the areas in the two censuses were not the same; some were affected by reclassification and annexation between censuses. As a result, five localities—namely, Thimi, Kirtipur, and Banepa in the hills, and Malangawa and Matihani in the terai—that were designated as urban in 1961 were reclassified or annexed to other localities in 1971. In contrast, five new areas—Bhadrapur, Hetauda, Bhairahwa, and Butwal in the terai, and Ilam in the hills—were newly classified as urban areas in the 1971 census. Map 4 shows these plus the rest of the urban areas as classified in the 1971 census. As of that period, most of the urban localities in Nepal were clustered in the central and eastern part of the country. This pattern of the growth of urban centers may be directly related to better transportation facilities in those regions.

Table 20 shows the distribution and growth of urban areas during 1961—71. In order to show the growth rate for each area, we present data only for localities that were classified as urban in both the 1961 and 1971 censuses. The data indicate that seven out of 11 urban areas had populations of over 20,000 as of 1971, and only Kathmandu had a population over 150,000. The three Kathmandu Valley cities—Kathmandu, Bhaktapur, and Lalitpur—represented 60 percent of the total urban population in 1961, and 54 percent in 1971.[38] This suggests that the primacy of the three cities has been declining over the years. The largest city outside Kathmandu Valley is Biratnagar, with

---

38 Bhaktapur and Lalitpur are also known as Bhadgaon and Patan, respectively.

MAP 4 Urban areas of Nepal: 1971 census

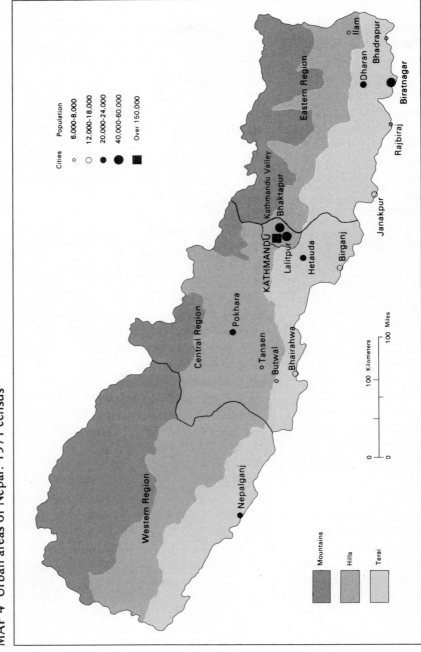

TABLE 20 Distribution and growth of urban areas: Nepal, 1961—71

Urban areas	Census population		% distribution of total urban population		Annual growth rate, 1961—71
	1961	1971	1961	1971	
Bhaktapur	33,877	40,112	10.1	8.7	1.7
Biratnagar	35,355	45,100	10.5	9.8	2.4
Birganj	10,769	12,999	3.2	2.8	1.9
Dharan	13,998	20,503	4.2	4.4	3.8
Janakpur	8,928	14,294	2.7	3.1	4.7
Kathmandu	121,019	150,402	36.1	32.6	2.2
Lalitpur	47,713	59,049	14.2	12.8	2.1
Nepalganj	15,817	23,523	4.7	5.1	4.0
Pokhara	5,413	20,611	1.6	4.5	13.4
Rajbiraj	5,232	7,832	1.6	1.7	4.1
Tansen	5,136	6,434	1.5	1.4	2.3
Total	303,257	400,859	90.4	86.9	2.8
All urban areas	336,222	461,938	100.0	100.0	3.2

NOTE: In order to estimate the growth rates for 1961—71, the table presents only those urban localities that were classified as urban in both the 1961 and 1971 censuses. Accordingly, the table represents 90 and 87 percent respectively of all population defined as urban in the 1961 and 1971 censuses.

SOURCES: The census population counts are from Nepal, CBS (1967, vol. 2; and 1975a: vol. 1, table 1).

a population of over 45,000 in 1971. This city has become a major industrial and commercial center.

The annual growth rates shown in Table 20 should be interpreted with caution, because they reflect not only natural increase, but also the effects of migration and reclassification. The censuses do not provide information on migration to and from urban areas, nor do they provide information on population added or lost owing to boundary changes. Nevertheless, if the growth rates are any indication of the pattern of urban growth in Nepal, it appears that the terai urban centers (see also Map 4) experienced higher growth rates during the decade than other cities (except Pokhara). Five terai urban areas—Biratnagar, Dharan, Janakpur, Nepalganj, and Rajbiraj—recorded an average of about 3.8 percent annual growth during 1961—71. The three cities in Kathmandu Valley experienced an average annual growth rate of 2.1 percent, which was nearly equal to the national population growth rate of 2.0 percent per annum during that decade.

Among the urban areas, Pokhara showed phenomenal growth, from just over 5,000 inhabitants in 1961 to almost 21,000 in 1971, implying an annual growth rate of 13.4 percent. A large share of this increase can probably be accounted for by changes in the municipal boundary during the intercensal period, but migration to Pokhara may have also been high, especially as new roads linked Pokhara with Kathmandu and the Indian border in the late 1960s.

Because more localities have been designated as urban since the 1971 census, we expect that a larger proportion of Nepal's population lives in urban areas now than in 1971. But was there a net flow of migrants from rural to urban areas during the 1970s? The Demographic Sample Survey of 1974–78 attempted to answer this question by monitoring migration streams to and from selected sample areas around the country (Bourini, 1976:23–25, 36–42; Bourini, 1977: 12–14, 25–32; Nepal, CBS, 1978:7–8, 20–27). Unfortunately, the published survey results appear to be internally inconsistent. For example, all three survey reports covering successive reinterviews estimated higher rates of urban out-migration than of urban in-migration for Kathmandu Valley urban areas, a result that suggests net out-migration from Kathmandu Valley cities in the 1970s. Yet, all three reports also estimated positive net in-migration for Kathmandu Valley urban areas, with no explanation of how these estimates were derived. Thus, the migration data from the DSS are not very helpful for monitoring migration trends during the 1970s.

Nepal has experienced slow urbanization in recent decades. One reason is that virgin lands in the terai have provided an outlet for the excess population in the hills and mountains. Rural-to-rural migration has been sustained by the availability of arable land in the terai. As acquisition of land in the terai becomes more difficult, rural-to-urban migration may begin, even if employment prospects in urban areas are not bright. Greater economic viability in hill and terai rural areas could help accommodate the population growth taking place and allow increases in per capita living standards in rural areas. Meanwhile, urban industrialization appropriate to Nepal's needs must accelerate, in order to provide jobs for the expanding labor force in urban areas, which will come both from urban natural increase and from rural-to-urban migration.

Migration from the hills and mountains has provided a safety valve for natural population increase in rural Nepal for decades, and to a lesser extent for more than a century. But Nepal's population is growing faster now. Neither the neighboring countries nor the Nepal terai can be expected to take increasing numbers of migrants from Nepal's hills and mountains in the future; already the terai areas are filling up with new settlers.

To summarize, Nepal is predominantly rural. Only a tiny proportion of the population is urban and the rate of urbanization has been slow. Yet internal and international migration have produced substantial population redistribution in Nepal. During the 1950s and earlier, people from the hills and mountains migrated from Nepal, mainly to India. Internal migration did not become an important component of population redistribution until the 1960s, after the government's anti-malaria campaign opened the sparsely inhabited terai to settlement. Responding to population pressure in the hills and mountains and to the opportunity of acquiring virgin land, inhabitants of the hills and mountains began moving into the terai. Thus the stream of internal migration was characterized by vertical movement; lateral movement was pronounced within the terai only. Migrants were predominantly male. The process of internal migration dampened the volume of migration abroad during the 1960s, but during the 1970s emigration may have once again become a salient feature of Nepal's population redistribution.

POPULATION AND THE ENVIRONMENT

Located on the slopes and in the foothills of the geologically young Himalayan mountain chain, Nepal is subject to a powerful natural erosion process because of the steepness of the terrain and because most of the annual rainfall comes in torrents during the summer months. The Himalayas are the world's youngest, tallest, and steepest mountains, composed of fragile sedimentary rock. Nepal is therefore one of the world's more delicate ecosystems. The forests growing on the hillsides help to hold the soil, retain moisture, and retard the erosion process. Where the forests have been destroyed, rain and melting snows have carried off the soil, depositing it at low altitudes; there excessive water runoff and siltation have caused the rivers to change course and flood their banks. Eckholm (1976:77) has observed that Nepal faces "the world's most acute national soil erosion problem." The environmental deterioration occurring now in Nepal is nothing new; it has been going on for centuries. But the current rate of deterioration is

new. In general, the reason for Nepal's erosion problems is rapid population growth without any basic changes in the traditional methods of
exploiting the environment for human use. Historically, people first
moved into the hills, cut or burned down a section of forest, then
planted crops and built houses on the cleared land. At first the land
was fertile, but as the topsoil eroded, crop yields declined. This development led the settlers to cut down more forest, often on steeper
slopes, and to plant more land per person, which contributed further
to the soil erosion. As the fields were destroyed by erosion, the people
moved on, abandoning their former lands and clearing a new forest
somewhere else. When the population of Nepal was small, the practice
of shifting cultivation did not cause critical environmental damage;
but now, combined with rapid population growth and high population
density on the arable lands in the hills, it has accelerated the speed of
environmental destruction. Some members of the Nepal National
Planning Commission fear that "the continuation of present trends
[of deforestation] may lead to the development of a semi-desert type
ecology in the hilly regions" (Eckholm, 1976:81).

Agriculture is not the only reason for the destruction of Nepal's
forests, however. The rapidly growing population also needs wood for
fuel. Eighty-seven percent of the country's energy consumption for
all purposes comes from firewood.[39] Because Nepal is at an early stage
of economic development, only 6 percent of the energy consumed is
used for industry or transport, whereas 93 percent is used for domestic purposes, which means cooking, heating, and lighting in private
homes. A tiny proportion of household energy needs is met by the
use of petroleum and electricity; the rest is met primarily by firewood,
and some comes from the burning of rice husks and animal dung.

Because Nepal's energy economy is almost totally dependent on
firewood, far more wood is cut each year than can be replenished by
natural forest growth. As of the mid-1970s, a sustainable level of
annual fuel wood production from Nepal's forests was estimated to be
about 78 kg. per capita; yet approximately 546 kg. of fuel wood per
capita were cut, about seven times the sustainable annual production.
The overcutting is occurring everywhere, but at a faster rate in the
hills and mountains than in the terai, and the destruction of the forests
is heightened by the practice of "tree mining," that is, cutting down

39 Information in this paragraph and the next is from Energy Research and Development Group (ERDG, 1976:76, 111–23) and Eckholm (1976:103).

all the trees closest to human settlements, rather than selective cutting throughout the forest. A common situation now is that all of the forest in a huge swath around each village or town settlement is gone, and someone from each family must walk half a day or more to the nearest source of wood to gather firewood. Just a generation ago the task might have taken only an hour or two.

A third reason for the destruction of Nepal's forests is the growing need for lumber for housing. Traditional housing is built of whole logs rather than sawed timber. Rieger (1976:19) has estimated that if wood were used efficiently in housing construction less than one-third of that now logged per house would be required.

Nepal's forests are also being devoured as animal fodder. A 1969 estimate of Nepal's livestock population was 6.2 million cows and oxen, 3.5 million water buffaloes, and 4.3 million sheep and goats (Panday, 1976:47). Almost all rural families in Nepal have one or several such large farm animals. Some fodder needs are met by crop residues and overgrazed pastures, but especially during the dry season the forests supply much of the fodder. Animals graze in the forests, eating not only grasses but also the young saplings. Farmers cut most of the leaves from the trees to feed their animals, thus weakening or killing trees that cannot tolerate such treatment.

Finally, for centuries handicraft and cottage industries have used wood from the forests (Acharya, 1976). Artisans have made household utensils and furniture from wood, using wasteful cutting techniques. Bronze metal workers, copper smelters, and blacksmiths have used large quantities of wood charcoal. The production of traditional Nepalese paper requires a special bark and much firewood. Nepal's handicraft industries use wood both as a raw material and as fuel.

In 1954, a United Nations forestry specialist warned that deforestation in the hills was "becoming catastrophic and erosion is causing the loss not only of property but also of human lives" (Eckholm, 1976: 80). Monitoring, mapping, and quantifying the loss of forests has proved difficult, but will be easier when satellite photographs of the country, taken in successive years, become available to scientists. The Nepal government is negotiating for access to such data from a new India-based LANDSAT satellite receiving station. Meanwhile, several estimates exist of Nepal's forest reserves. A Forest Resources Survey in 1964 using aerial photographs indicated that 45.5 percent of Nepal's total land area was in forest at that time; 24.3 percent was covered with "noncommercial" forests (that is, inaccessible forests in subalpine, steep, or rocky terrain, and forests reduced to scrub and shrubs by encroachment) and 21.2 percent was still forested with "commercial" (that is, accessible and exploitable) forests (ERDG, 1976:113). It is primarily the commercial forests that have been exploited since 1964. The hills and mountains had about 1.7 million hectares (4.1 million acres) of commercial forest in 1964; estimates of the remaining commercial forest area as of 1975 range from 1.0 to 1.5 million hectares. The terai and inner terai had about 1.3 million hectares of commercial forest as of 1964; as of the mid-1970s the remaining commercial forest land there was variously estimated to comprise between 0.5 and 1.1 million hectares, depending on the estimation technique used (ERDG, 1976:115). In 1976 the Energy Research and Development Group projected that, if the current rate of forest encroachment continued, the accessible forests of Nepal would be virtually gone in less than 20 years (ERDG, 1976:121–23).

Long before then, of course, the destructive effects of deforestation will be even more evident than they are already. The loss of forest cover is causing devastating erosion in many parts of Nepal. Observers have noted with irony that Nepal's most precious export, for which it receives no compensation, is topsoil. An estimated 240 million cubic meters of soil are lost every year (IBRD, 1974: annex 6:2). The decline in crop yields is a direct result. Interviews with farmers in one upper hill district elicited the following comments on the situation:

Some 30 years ago we still produced enough grain to allow us to exchange surplus for necessary daily goods, which we could not get from our farming. Of the grains harvested, one-third was exchanged. . . . While the good farmers who have enough cattle and do very intensive cultivation can still increase their yields, this is not the general trend. In a *khet* [low land] where we sowed 4 *mana* [1 mana = 33 cu. inches] of seed we used to get one *muri* [1 muri = 160 manas] of paddy; now we need an area with 8 mana of seed to get one muri. Our wheat used to have big ears and long halms and we filled six baskets (*doko*) a day; nowadays it is sometimes only one or two. In many houses there is no longer enough food. For some the harvest grains are sufficient for only three—four months a year. Why is there a decrease in yield?—It has just happened, we don't know why. We just get less even if we put in the same efforts. The rain washes away the most fertile topsoil every year. So we have to plough into the new unfertile soil every year (Chhetri et al., 1976:160—61).

The end result of this process of erosion and declining yields is that cultivation ceases on the most eroded land. It was estimated in the late 1960s, for example, that in Nepal's eastern hills as much as 38 percent of the land area consisted of abandoned fields (India, Department of Agriculture, 1967:5).

Erosion is not always a gradual process. During the monsoon rains, hillsides unprotected by forests may give way all at once. These landslides can be extremely dangerous. A 1974–75 study of one central Nepal valley of about 20,000 people, for instance, reported on the effects of landslides in the valley's villages, which are located on steep hillsides:

In addition to the natural erosion in the last twenty years has come an erosion directly linked to the demographic pressure. In its total length a considerable number of landslides can be seen in Ankhu Khola valley today, some of which are two to three kilometers wide. . . . Each year, these slides get bigger. They cause considerable damage, carrying away fields, livestock and sometimes people and houses. In Lindjyo, a village of the upper valley, the slides caused so many deaths that the inhabitants were forced to move out and rebuild their village on the opposite side (Toffin, 1976:40).

Erosion and landslides fill up the rivers with heavy loads of silt. As the rivers reach the terai and India, they flow more slowly and drop much of the silt, which raises the river beds. River beds in the terai are rising at the rate of about 15–30 centimeters (6 inches to 1 foot) a year (Nepal, National Planning Commission, 1974b). The siltation in turn causes increased flooding during the monsoon rains, changes in river courses, and damage to irrigation structures and settlements. The final resting place of much of the silt load is the Bay of Bengal (see Map 1), where in 1974 an Earth Resources Technology Satellite spotted an immense new island just surfacing. It turned out to consist of 116,000 sq. km. of Himalayan silt (Sterling, 1976:14).

Thus, Nepal's rapid population growth, in combination with traditional practices in agriculture and in the household, has generated increased demand for cultivable acreage and firewood, which has led to a faster rate of environmental deterioration in recent decades. The worsening environmental deterioration, in turn, is causing hunger and a general decline in the economic situation of families; it necessitates greater physical work with less satisfactory results; it causes destruction of farmsteads, human dislocation, and even death; and it is weakening Nepal's agricultural base, from which the country's much larger future population will need to be fed.

The magnitude of the problems Nepal faces calls for innovative development approaches. During recent decades, some attempts at economic development in Nepal have been pursued without much understanding of the detrimental environmental effects these projects might have. The government of Nepal recognized the urgent need for an eco-logically sound development program during the 1970s, but the prac-ticalities of designing and implementing such a development path are only beginning to be worked out. Much has been learned from the unanticipated environmental consequences of projects previously thought to be suitable to Nepal's environment. During the 1950s and 1960s, for example, the Jiri Multipurpose Development Project, a joint Nepalese-Swiss project, was started and expanded in a remote valley seven days by foot from Kathmandu (Schmid, 1976). At first, the project bred improved water buffaloes for milk and cheese produc-tion. But the shortage of high-quality fodder for the water buffaloes soon became critical, and this problem could not be solved without a more comprehensive local development project, which was tried dur-ing the late 1960s. From their experiences, participants in the Jiri Project made the following recommendations for future development projects in the hill areas of Nepal. First, no development project should start without a basic ecological survey of the affected area. Second, a sectoral approach to development in the hills should be avoided and an integrated development approach taken. Third, project designs should allow for constant feedback, evaluation, and adjust-ment to unanticipated environmental effects as they become apparent. Fourth, efforts to develop a hill area should be accompanied by a motorable road between the development area and outside potential markets. This last observation is still a matter of intense debate in Nepal as the impact of road building is not always favorable.[40]

To lessen the pressure on Nepal's environment, one of the most ur-gent needs is for substitutes for fuel wood as an energy source. The country cannot maintain the present subsistence living level of its people without effective energy substitutes, much less carry out sig-nificant economic development. So far no commercially exploitable sources of fossil fuels (coal, oil, or natural gas) have been discovered in Nepal, though geological exploration is continuing (ERDG, 1976: 124–28). The country has enormous known hydropower potential. Large hydropower projects are prospective energy sources for meeting Nepal's long-term energy needs, but locations for them must be chosen carefully because they are likely to inundate large areas of

40 Schroeder and Sisler (1970), Rana (1971), and Blaikie et al. (1976) have at-
    tempted to assess the positive and negative effects of road building in Nepal.

farmland above the dams. Design of the dams needs to take into account the heavy silt loads that the rivers carry, seismic activity in the area, monsoon rains, and other peculiarities of the environment (ERDG, 1976:98–110). A few large hydropower stations may be appropriate in some parts of the country, whereas in others mini-hydropower projects may be preferable, to reduce transmission costs. Small hydropower stations can be built more quickly than large ones, and their environmental impact is more predictable.

Nepal's solar energy potential is also high (ERDG, 1976:150–55). Solar cookers, solar irrigation pumps, solar grain and fruit drying machines, and solar water heaters are all technically feasible now. The main constraint on their use is the current cost of importing such devices; part of Nepal's industrialization program might be to produce the simplest and cheapest possible solar devices for local use.

In addition to hydropower and solar energy, a third promising energy source is biogas derived from cattle and other animal dung (ERDG, 1976:128–49). Countries like India, China, and some Pacific islands are already using this energy source. A by-product of biogas derived from dung is fertilizer that is more nutrient-rich than the original dung. But the design and maintenance of biogas converters will be difficult in Nepal. This method of producing energy works best in hot climates and may not be suitable for higher altitudes in Nepal. Besides, biogas converters require frequent maintenance to work efficiently. If Nepal is going to produce energy from biogas, it will need to design and produce biogas converters suitable for each terrain and train local people to maintain them.

For each of these recommended energy sources—hydropower, solar, and biogas—the original capital costs are high per unit of energy output, but thereafter the energy source is inexpensive or free. One beneficial use for foreign aid in Nepal is to subsidize the introduction of these energy sources as alternatives to fuel wood.

The introduction of such energy sources in agricultural areas should be coordinated with the development of small-scale industries, powered by the new energy sources, that can generate increased income for the localities. Unless the poorer families in the villages experience rising incomes, they will continue to cut down trees in order to get free fuel, no matter what energy sources are available in their villages at some cost to the users.

Once an alternative energy source is available in an area, intensive reforestation will have a chance of succeeding. Emphasis in reforestation should be placed on trees having multiple uses, such as fruit trees, nut trees, high-yielding fodder trees, and medicinal plants. Reforestation has to be a community endeavor and responsibility. An educational campaign would probably be necessary to persuade villagers of the importance of trees for holding the soil, and how tree crops will materially benefit all the people in the village. If a major reforestation drive is attempted under present economic conditions, or in a way that benefits only the elite, the small trees might be stripped of leaves for fodder and cut down for fuel before they could grow.

To prevent further deforestation, alternative fodder sources must be found for livestock. There is no easy solution to this problem, for much former pasture land has had to be taken over for agriculture. If agricultural yields from good agricultural land can be increased substantially in hill and terai areas, it may be possible to take marginal land out of agriculture and devote it to raising fodder crops. Ways must be found for limiting the use of fodder to the land's sustainable yield.

Nepal's environmental situation is worsening. Although intensified exploitation of Nepal's resources is needed to provide adequately for the current and future population, deterioration of the environment must simultaneously be controlled, not only for the sake of Nepal's present and future citizens, but also for the people of the entire region. Part of the long-term solution to this dilemma lies in controlling the rapid population growth now taking place in Nepal.

FUTURE POPULATION PROSPECTS

For planning purposes, it is helpful to have estimates of likely population trends for the period under consideration, because actual trends affect every aspect of a development plan. We have therefore made three population projections for Nepal to the year 2030 based on different assumptions about the course of fertility and mortality over the 50-year period.

All of the projections begin with a population age and sex structure derived from the Nepal Fertility Survey household survey, corrected for age misreporting (see Table 2) and inflated to an estimated total population size of 13.8 million for mid-year 1976. We derived the total population figure by assuming that the 1971 census was undercounted by 5 percent, and that the population grew by 2.5 percent a year during the early 1970s.[41]

The projections assume a mortality level in 1976 of 11, based on the Coale-Demeny West model life tables (Coale and Demeny, 1966). Level 11 is the closest match to Nepal's mortality situation, because it implies an expectation of life at birth of 43.5 years and an infant mortality rate of 159. Age-specific and total fertility rates for 1976 are taken from NFS data for 1971–75; total fertility is assumed to be 6.2 births per woman at the beginning of the projection period. The techniques as described in Bogue and Rehling (1974) have been used for the projections.

All three projections begin with an estimated crude birth rate of 46.8, crude death rate of 20.9, and natural population increase rate of 25.9 per thousand population for 1976, estimates that our analysis indicates to be plausible. Because we cannot adequately assess likely international migration trends for the next 50 years, we assume that the natural population increase rate is equal to the population growth rate, and ignore the possible effects of international migration. The first projection, which we call the pessimistic projection, assumes that through the year 2030, both mortality and fertility decline, but at a slow rate. Expectation of life at birth is assumed to increase from 43.5 years in 1976 to 53.4 years in the year 2000 and 65.5 years in 2030 (or from model life table West level 11 to level 15 in the year 2000, and to level 20 in the year 2030). The total fertility rate is assumed to decrease from 6.2 births per woman in 1976 to 5.0 in 2000, and to 4.0 in 2030. Age-specific fertility rates for the years 2000 and 2030 are modeled on Sri Lanka's 1963 and 1970 age-specific fertility patterns (Sri Lanka, Department of Census and Statistics, 1978:90), because Nepal is more likely to follow a South Asian pattern of fertility change than a pattern found elsewhere.

The second, or optimistic, projection assumes that both mortality and fertility began to decline rapidly after 1976 and that this trend of steady, fast improvement will continue to the year 2030. We have designed this projection to meet the demographic targets proposed by Nepal's government in its drafted long-term health plan dated October 1974 (American Public Health Association, 1979:59). The government

---

41 An analysis of the 1971 census data has estimated an undercount of about 5 percent (see Kramer, 1979).

aims at reducing Nepal's crude birth rate to 25 per thousand in the
year 1995, and its population growth rate to 15 per thousand that
same year. For this projection, we assume that Nepal's expectation of
life at birth will rise from 43.5 years in 1976 to 61.8 years in 2000,
and to 75.7 years in 2030 (or from model life table West level 11 in
1976 to level 18.5 in the year 2000 and to level 24 in 2030). If this
mortality improvement were achieved, it would constitute faster mortality decline than Nepal has experienced thus far. We also assume
that the total fertility rate of 6.2 births per woman in 1976 will decline to only 2.2 births per woman in the year 2000, equivalent to
replacement-level fertility. Such an extremely rapid fertility decline
would be required for Nepal to achieve its stated 1995 fertility target.
Assuming that if such success were achieved prior to the year 2000,
further fertility reduction might also be possible, we project a decline
in total fertility to only 1.0 birth per woman in the year 2030 for the
completion of the optimistic projection. Because no South Asian
country has achieved replacement fertility, we use an idealized model
of age-specific fertility that seems appropriate to South Asian experience so far. It is called the "broad peak low fertility model"
(United Nations, ESA, 1965:110).

Both the pessimistic and the optimistic projections assume that
Nepal will experience a continuous trend for over 50 years, and that
the trend has already begun. Because conditions in the real world
rarely remain constant over 50 years, a more realistic projection
would include discontinuities. For example, one might posit a disaster
model, in which environmental deterioration in Nepal is not arrested
but rather accelerates, health and nutritional levels worsen greatly, per
capita income declines drastically, the economy and political system
break down, civil or international war occurs, there are sharp rises in
mortality at all ages, and fertility declines only temporarily in response
to famine, only to rise once again to the previous level. Another dis-
continuous scenario, which we believe is more likely to happen, is il-
lustrated by the third projection, which we term the turning point
projection. In this model, we assume that mortality and fertility follow our pessimistic projection, until some point when the populace
and the government become able to bring about rapid mortality and
fertility decline. After that point, which might be in 1985 or 1990 or
some later time, mortality and fertility might begin dropping at the
speed simulated in our optimistic projection. Many other countries

have experienced abrupt accelerations in their mortality or fertility declines, or in both. The turning point projection assumes that Nepal's rapid mortality and fertility declines will begin in 1985. Before then, demographic change is assumed to be slow, with the expectation of life at birth rising from 43.5 years in 1976 to 47.2 years in 1985, and with the total fertility rate declining from 6.2 births per woman in 1976 to 5.7 in 1985. After 1985, rapid improvement is assumed, expectation of life at birth rising to 59.4 years in 2000 and to 73.0 years in 2030, and the total fertility rate dropping to 3.4 in 2000 and to 1.5 in 2030. The mortality change is equivalent to a shift from level 11 (of West model life tables) in 1976 to level 12.5 in 1985, to level 17.5 in the year 2000, and to level 23 in 2030. Age-specific fertility rates are modeled on Nepal's 1971—75 fertility pattern for 1976 and 1985, Sri Lanka's 1974 fertility level and pattern for the year 2000 (Sri Lanka, Department of Census and Statistics, 1978:98), and the broad peak low fertility model for 2030 (United Nations, ESA, 1965:110).

The turning point projection makes assumptions similar to those of the optimistic projection except that the beginning of rapid demographic change lags nine years behind that of the optimistic projection. The choice of 1985 as the turning point year is obviously arbitrary; such a demographic shift might begin at any time or might not happen at all.

Results of the three projections are presented in Tables 21 and 22. The projected total population size for 1976 through 2026 is shown in Figure 9. Nepal in 1976 had about 42 percent of its population in the age groups 0—14, a high child dependency burden (Table 21). According to the pessimistic projection, Nepal's age structure would change little over the 50-year projection period. In the year 2026 the country would still have about 38 percent of its population under age 15. In contrast, the optimistic projection would produce a marked shift in Nepal's age structure to an older pattern characteristic of low fertility countries. The turning point projection would lead to an age structure older than that of the pessimistic projection and younger than that of the optimistic projection.

The projections indicate that Nepal will experience rapid population growth in the coming decades even if it succeeds in achieving the long-term health plan targets and low fertility by the year 2000. Nepal's population size will increase from about 13.8 million in 1976 to between 21.8 and 25.1 million by the turn of the century, according

TABLE 21 Three projections of the age structure of Nepal: 1976–2026
(Proportions in percentages, total population in thousands)

Age group	1976	1981	1986	1991	1996	2001	2006	2011	2016	2021	2026
Pessimistic projection											
0–14	42	43	43	43	42	41	40	40	39	39	38
15–64	55	54	54	54	54	56	57	57	58	58	58
65 and over	3	3	3	3	3	3	3	3	3	4	4
Total population	13,793	15,696	17,819	20,174	22,779	25,680	28,970	32,720	36,942	41,612	46,705
Optimistic projection											
0–14	42	42	41	39	36	31	27	24	22	20	18
15–64	55	55	56	58	61	65	68	71	72	72	73
65 and over	3	3	3	4	4	4	5	5	6	7	9
Total population	13,793	15,596	17,401	19,143	20,728	22,039	23,257	24,424	25,425	26,157	26,565
Turning point projection											
0–14	42	43	43	42	40	37	33	31	29	27	25
15–64	55	54	54	54	56	60	63	65	66	67	69
65 and over	3	3	3	3	3	4	4	4	5	5	6
Total population	13,793	15,702	17,832	20,022	22,163	24,178	26,239	28,395	30,516	32,421	33,952

NOTE: Some percentages do not sum to 100 because of rounding.

TABLE 22 Results of alternate population projections: Nepal, 1976–2030

Year	Pessimistic projection				Optimistic projection				Turning point projection			
	CBR	CDR	NIR	Size (1000s)	CBR	CDR	NIR	Size (1000s)	CBR	CDR	NIR	Size (1000s)
1976	46.8	20.9	25.9	13,793	46.8	20.9	25.9	13,793	46.8	20.9	25.9	13,793
1977	46.4	20.5	25.9	14,157	45.6	20.2	25.4	14,152	46.5	20.5	26.0	14,157
1978	46.0	20.2	25.8	14,529	44.3	19.5	24.8	14,511	46.1	20.2	25.9	14,530
1979	45.6	19.9	25.7	14,909	43.1	18.8	24.3	14,872	45.7	19.9	25.8	14,912
1980	45.1	19.5	25.6	15,299	41.9	18.1	23.8	15,234	45.3	19.5	25.8	15,302
1981	44.7	19.2	25.5	15,696	40.7	17.4	23.3	15,596	44.8	19.2	25.6	15,702
1982	44.3	18.8	25.5	16,103	39.5	16.8	22.7	15,959	44.4	18.8	25.6	16,110
1983	43.8	18.5	25.3	16,518	38.4	16.1	22.3	16,321	44.0	18.5	25.5	16,528
1984	43.4	18.1	25.3	16,943	37.2	15.5	21.7	16,682	43.6	18.1	25.5	16,956
1985	42.9	17.7	25.2	17,376	36.1	14.9	21.2	17,042	43.1	17.8	25.3	17,393
1986	42.5	17.4	25.1	17,819	34.9	14.3	20.6	17,401	41.8	17.1	24.7	17,832
1987	42.0	17.0	25.0	18,271	33.8	13.7	20.1	17,757	40.5	16.3	24.2	18,272
1988	41.5	16.7	24.8	18,733	32.6	13.2	19.4	18,110	39.2	15.7	23.5	18,711
1989	41.1	16.3	24.8	19,204	31.5	12.6	18.9	18,459	38.0	15.0	23.0	19,149
1990	40.6	16.0	24.6	19,684	30.4	12.1	18.3	18,804	36.7	14.3	22.4	19,586
1991	40.2	15.7	24.5	20,174	29.3	11.7	17.6	19,143	35.5	13.7	21.8	20,022
1992	39.7	15.3	24.4	20,674	28.2	11.2	17.0	19,476	34.4	13.1	21.3	20,456
1993	39.3	15.0	24.3	21,184	27.1	10.8	16.3	19,802	33.2	12.5	20.7	20,888
1994	38.9	14.7	24.2	21,705	26.0	10.4	15.6	20,120	32.1	12.0	20.1	21,317
1995	38.5	14.4	24.1	22,237	24.9	10.0	14.9	20,429	31.0	11.5	19.5	21,742

TABLE 22 *(continued)*

Year	Pessimistic projection				Optimistic projection				Turning point projection			
	CBR	CDR	NIR	Size (1000s)	CBR	CDR	NIR	Size (1000s)	CBR	CDR	NIR	Size (1000s)
1996	38.2	14.1	24.1	22,779	23.9	9.6	14.0	20,728	29.9	11.0	18.9	22,163
1997	37.8	13.8	24.0	22,334	22.8	9.3	13.5	21,015	28.9	10.5	18.4	22,578
1998	37.5	13.6	23.9	23,901	21.6	9.0	12.6	21,291	27.8	10.1	17.7	22,988
1999	37.2	13.3	23.9	24,480	20.5	8.7	11.8	21,552	26.7	9.6	17.1	23,390
2000	36.9	13.0	23.9	25,073	19.4	8.4	11.0	21,798	25.7	9.3	16.4	23,784
2001	36.7	12.8	23.9	25,680	19.2	8.3	10.9	22,039	25.5	9.1	16.4	24,178
2002	36.5	12.5	24.0	26,303	19.1	8.1	11.0	22,281	25.3	8.9	16.4	24,578
2003	36.4	12.3	24.1	26,944	18.9	8.0	10.9	22,525	25.1	8.7	16.4	24,985
2004	36.2	12.1	24.1	27,601	18.6	7.9	10.7	22,770	24.9	8.6	16.3	25,398
2005	36.0	11.9	24.1	28,277	18.4	7.8	10.6	23,014	24.7	8.5	16.2	25,816
2006	35.9	11.7	24.2	28,970	18.1	7.7	10.4	23,257	24.5	8.3	16.2	26,239
2007	35.7	11.4	24.3	29,682	17.8	7.6	10.2	23,498	24.3	8.2	16.1	26,665
2008	35.5	11.2	24.3	30,413	17.5	7.6	9.9	23,736	24.0	8.1	15.9	27,095
2009	35.4	11.0	24.4	31,163	17.1	7.5	9.6	23,970	23.7	7.9	15.8	27,528
2010	35.2	10.8	24.4	31,932	16.8	7.4	9.4	24,200	23.3	7.8	15.5	27,961
2011	35.0	10.6	24.4	32,720	16.4	7.3	9.1	24,424	23.0	7.7	15.3	28,395
2012	34.8	10.4	24.4	33,527	15.9	7.3	8.6	24,641	22.5	7.6	14.9	28,827
2013	34.5	10.2	24.3	34,353	15.5	7.2	8.3	24,851	22.1	7.5	14.6	29,257
2014	34.3	10.0	24.3	35,197	15.0	7.1	7.9	25,052	21.6	7.4	14.2	29,683
2015	34.0	9.9	24.1	36,060	14.5	7.1	7.4	25,243	21.1	7.3	13.8	30,103

Year	CBR	CDR	NIR	Population	CBR	CDR	NIR	Population	CBR	CDR	NIR	Population
2016	33.7	9.7	24.0	36,942	14.0	7.1	6.9	25,425	20.5	7.1	13.4	30,516
2017	33.5	9.5	24.0	37,841	13.4	7.0	6.4	25,595	20.0	7.0	13.0	30,920
2018	33.2	9.3	23.9	38,768	12.9	7.0	5.9	25,754	19.4	7.0	12.4	31,314
2019	32.9	9.1	23.8	39,692	12.4	7.0	5.4	25,901	18.7	6.9	11.8	31,697
2020	32.5	9.0	23.5	40,643	11.9	7.0	4.9	26,036	18.1	6.8	11.3	32,066
2021	32.2	8.8	23.4	41,612	11.3	7.0	4.3	26,157	17.4	6.7	10.7	32,421
2022	31.9	8.6	23.3	42,597	10.8	7.0	3.8	26,266	16.8	6.7	10.1	32,761
2023	31.6	8.5	23.1	43,599	10.3	7.0	3.3	26,361	16.1	6.6	9.5	33,085
2024	31.3	8.3	23.0	44,617	9.8	7.0	2.8	26,442	15.5	6.6	8.9	33,392
2025	31.0	8.1	22.9	45,653	9.4	7.1	2.3	26,510	14.8	6.5	8.3	33,681
2026	30.7	8.0	22.7	46,705	8.9	7.2	1.7	26,565	14.2	6.5	7.7	33,952
2027	30.4	7.9	22.5	47,775	8.5	7.2	1.3	26,606	13.6	6.5	7.1	34,205
2028	30.1	7.7	22.4	48,862	8.1	7.3	0.8	26,634	13.0	6.5	6.5	34,439
2029	29.8	7.6	22.2	49,967	7.7	7.4	0.3	26,648	12.4	6.5	5.9	34,654
2030	29.6	7.4	22.2	51,090	7.3	7.5	-0.2	26,650	11.9	6.6	5.3	34,851

CBR—crude birth rate per thousand.
CDR—crude death rate per thousand.
NIR—natural increase rate per thousand.

FIGURE 9   Three projections of the population size of Nepal:
1976—2026

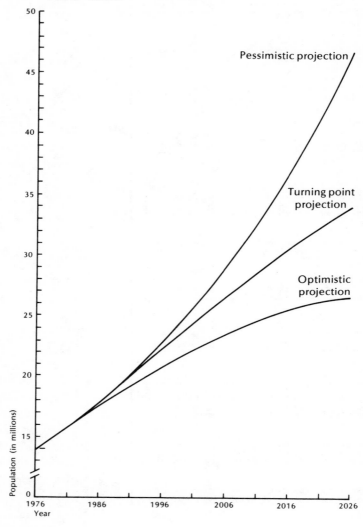

SOURCE: Table 21.

to our alternate projections (Table 22). The country will need to develop its economy enough during this decade and the next to provide
basic subsistence needs for a substantially larger population.

The achievement of urgent priorities will be made more difficult by the rapid increase in population. The provision of universal elementary and secondary education, for example, will require much greater effort than heretofore because of the larger size of the population under age 15. After decades of struggle to increase the population's level of educational attainment, the government has made concrete progress. By 1971, 24 percent of boys and 7 percent of girls in the age group 6–14 were enrolled in school (Nepal, CBS, 1977:139); and those proportions have undoubtedly increased since the 1971 census was taken. Because Nepal's population is young and the school enrollment rate is still low, the drive toward universal school enrollment of children would consume perhaps a fourth of Nepal's development funds in the coming decades even without the rapid population growth ahead. But in addition, the number of persons in the 6–14 age group is expected to increase by 38 percent between 1976 and 2000, according even to the optimistic projection. If the pessimistic projection prevailed, the population in that age group would increase by 82 percent over the same period. The number of persons 6–14 would increase by 69 percent between 1976 and 2000 in the turning point projection.

The rapid increase in the number of persons in the prime working ages during the next few decades is likely to exacerbate problems of unemployment and underemployment in the coming decades. According to a recent survey (Nepal, National Planning Commission Secretariat, 1978:57–63), as of 1977, approximately 6 percent of males and of females in Nepal's rural labor force were unemployed; in urban areas, 5 percent of males and 10 percent of females in the labor force were unemployed. Underemployment was also widespread. The survey calculated that employed workers in rural areas worked only 37 percent of the working days in 1977; female workers experienced more underemployment than male workers. In urban areas employed workers actually worked only 55 percent of the working days. All three of our projections indicate that the number of persons of working age (15–64) will increase by over 80 percent between 1976 and the year 2000.

Though all three scenarios produce rapid population growth between now and the turn of the century, the optimistic one, if it could be achieved, would eventually result in a much smaller stationary population size than the pessimistic one. The rapid fertility decline modeled in the optimistic projection, culminating in the total fertility rate of only 1.0 child per woman in the year 2030, could produce zero population growth by that year. Nepal could, if it followed our most optimistic assumptions, achieve a stationary population of about 26.7 million persons, almost twice the size of the estimated 1976 population, by the time population growth ceased.

In contrast, the pessimistic projection results in a population of 51.1 million persons by the year 2030, or 3.7 times the estimated 1976 population; and the population would still be growing at over 2 percent annually. The transition from high mortality and high fertility would be only partly completed, so that rapid population growth would continue throughout most of the twenty-first century if fertility and mortality continued their slow decline. Nepal's eventual stationary population size would be many times the stationary population achieved under the assumptions of the optimistic projection.

For the turning point projection we assumed that Nepal would not begin rapid demographic progress until 1985. Between 1976 and 1985, much precious time would be lost. Even though demographic change would be rapid under the turning point projection after 1985, by the turn of the century, Nepal's population size would be perhaps two million persons larger than under the optimistic projection, and would still be growing faster. By the year 2030, the turning point scenario would result in a population of 34.9 million, 2.5 times that of 1976, and the population would still be growing slowly in size. Nepal therefore cannot afford to postpone completion of its demographic transition. Rapid fertility decline must begin soon if future population growth is to be contained.

Unfortunately, Nepal is at such an early stage of its demographic transition that at least three decades of rapid population growth lie immediately ahead. The country's arable land is already densely populated and has sustained much environmental destruction, some of which may prove irreversible. Yet, Nepal has one advantage in being a latecomer to demographic, economic, and social development, for it can learn from the experiences and innovations of more developed countries. It is possible that Nepal's fertility transition will be surprisingly rapid once it begins. Even so, the demographic momentum inherent in its current age structure will result in at least a doubling of the population size before it reaches zero population growth.

GLOSSARY OF TECHNICAL TERMS

age heaping. *See* heaping.

age-sex structure. The composition of a population as determined by the number or proportion of males and females in each age category. The age-sex structure of a population is the cumulative result of past trends in fertility, mortality, and migration.

age-specific fertility rate. The average annual number of births to women in a given age group during a specified period of time per thousand women in the same age group, based on the mid-period population.

age truncation. The lack of retrospective data for women at the oldest reproductive ages in prior years, due to the fact that only women currently 15—49 years old are asked for pregnancy history data.

anthropometric. Relating to the science of measuring the human body and its parts and functional capacities, as an aid to the study of variations among people.

Ayurvedic. A system of medicine originating in India, the principles and treatments of which were first summarized and compiled in written form in the seventh century B.C. Ayurvedic theories of pathology are based on humoral disequilibrium. Treatments rely largely on herbs and precious metals.

census. A canvass of a given area, resulting in an enumeration of the entire population and the compilation of demographic, social, and economic information pertaining to that population at a specified time.

census survival ratios. Based on two censuses x years apart, the proportion of persons enumerated at age a in the first census who survive to be counted at age $a + x$ in the second census.

BCG immunization. Bacillus Calmette-Guérin vaccine, a vaccine prepared from a living attenuated strain of tubercle bacilli and used to vaccinate humans against tuberculosis.

children ever born. The number of live births a woman has had, regardless of whether the children are now living or dead, living with their mother or away from her. These data are collected only from ever married women, on the assumption that never married women have had no births, and then averaged over all women in a particular age group.

closed birth interval. The interval between one live birth and a succeeding live birth.

cohort. A group of individuals who experience the same event in the same time period, such as birth or marriage in the same year.

completed fertility. The total number of live births per woman experienced by the end of the childbearing years.

crude birth rate (CBR). The average annual number of births during a specified period of time per thousand persons (based on the mid-period population).

crude death rate (CDR). The average annual number of deaths during a specified period of time per thousand persons (based on the mid-period population).

cumulative fertility rate (CFR). As used here, the sum of the age-specific fertility rates up to a given age of women, applicable to a specified period of time or point in time.

de jure population count. A population count in which individuals are attributed to a geographical area by virtue of their usual place of residence, whether or not they were actually located in that area at the time of the enumeration.

demographic transition. The shift from a traditional pattern of relatively high mortality and fertility to a modern pattern of relatively low mortality and fertility. Because the decline in mortality usually precedes the decline in fertility, there is an interim period of rapid natural population increase during the transition period.

demography. The scientific study of human populations, including their size, composition, distribution, density, and growth, along with the relationships between population processes and other socioeconomic characteristics of the population.

disease prevalence. The number of persons who have a certain disease at a given time per population at risk.

effective marriage. In Nepal, the occasion when a formally married couple begins cohabiting, usually after the wife's menarche.

endemic disease. A disease that is native to and constantly present in a particular place.

expectation of life at birth (e_0). The average number of years a person could expect to live after being born alive, if mortality conditions stayed the same as those found at each age in a given year.

fecundity. The physiological capacity to produce a live child, including the capacity of a man or woman to contribute to conception, the capacity of a couple to conceive, and the capacity of a woman to carry a fetus to a live birth once it is conceived.

fertility. Actual reproductive performance of individuals, couples, or populations.

heaping. The tendency of respondents or enumerators to favor certain numbers, usually those ending in zero or five, and to avoid other numbers when reporting age, year of birth, duration of marriage, etc.

hypo-protein edema. Fluid retention and swelling in the body caused by protein deficiency.

hypothetical cohort. A demographic construct that is used to infer the experience of a cohort of people as they move through life from the experiences of people of different ages at a particular time.

incidence (of a disease). The number of persons contracting a disease during a given time period per population at risk.

index of age preference. A summary measure of the extent of age heaping observed in a particular census or survey.

infant mortality rate (IMR). A measure of the frequency of deaths experienced during a specified time period by infants between the moment of their live birth and the attainment of exact age one. Usually calculated as the number of deaths to infants under one year of age per thousand live births occurring during the same calendar year.

kwashiorkor. Severe malnutrition in infants and children that is characterized by failure to grow and develop, changes in the pigmentation of the skin and hair, edema, fatty degeneration of the liver, anemia, and apathy. Caused by a diet excessively high in carbohydrate and extremely low in protein.

life table. A tabular display of the expectation of life at each age and the probability of dying at each age for a given population, according to the age-specific death rates prevailing at one particular time. The life table gives an organized, complete picture of a population's mortality.

lifetime internal migration. Migration within a country by persons born in one location and residing at another location at the time of a census or survey, regardless of all intervening moves.

migrant. A person who moves across a specified boundary and sets up a new permanent or temporary residence for a long enough period to be classified a resident at destination.

model life table. A life table that does not display the observed mortality of an actual population, but rather is a composite life table derived from mortality experience in many populations or one population at different points in time.

model stable age-sex structure. The age and sex structure characteristic of a model stable population.

model stable population. A population that has been subject to a fixed schedule of age-specific fertility rates and a fixed schedule of age-specific mortality rates for an indefinite period of time without migration.

natural population increase rate. The increase rate per thousand population that results solely from an excess of births over deaths and does not take migration into account. Crude birth rate minus crude death rate equals crude rate of natural increase.

Nepalization. The attempt, in all Nepal but especially in the terai and inner terai, to increase the proportion of the population and the political and economic power of that sector of the population born in Nepal and with a Nepalese, as distinct from an Indian or other foreign, cultural identity.

nitrogen-fixing crops. Crops that convert inorganic nitrogen, such as that found in air, into nitrogen fertilizer assimilable by subsequent crops grown on that land.

nuptiality. The frequency, characteristics, and dissolution of marriages and other stable sexual unions in a population.

open birth interval. The length of time that has elapsed between the last live birth and the date of enquiry.

parity. The number of live births a woman has had.

population growth rate. The annual percentage increase in the size of a population resulting from births, deaths, and net migration in the population.

postenumeration matching check or matching survey. A small, intensive survey that follows a large survey or census and attempts to estimate the extent of error, particularly the net undercount, in the main enumeration by matching persons enumerated at both times and assuming that the nonmatched cases are indicative of the net coverage error.

pregnancy history. An account gathered for individual women of all pregnancies they have ever had, with the dates of the beginning and end of each one and its outcome (whether it terminated in a live birth or a fetal death). Additional details may be included, such as date of marriage, length of lactation, occurrence of infant or child death, and whether any abortions were spontaneous or induced.

prevalence (of a disease). The number of persons who have a particular disease at a given time per population at risk; includes new cases and continuing cases.

pull factors. Perceived advantages of a certain destination from the perspective of a potential migrant.

push factors. Perceived disadvantages of a point of origin that contribute to a potential migrant's decision to leave.

quasi-stable population analysis. A method of demographic analysis based on a model population that has not been subjected to migration, in which fertility has remained constant over a long period of time and mortality has been declining.

reference period error. A type of response error that is assumed to occur because respondents, when answering a question, have in mind a longer or shorter period of time than that designated in the question.

replacement level fertility. The level of fertility at which women on average have only enough daughters to replace themselves in the population over time.

sample survey. A survey in which only a portion, and not the whole population, is surveyed.

sampling error. The difference between a population value and an estimate of the value, derived from a random sample, that results because only a sample of values is observed. Sampling error is distinct from errors due to imperfect selection, bias in response or estimation, errors of observation and recording, etc. The totality of sampling errors in all possible samples of the same size generates the sampling distribution of the statistic that is used to estimate the population value.

sampling unit. One of the units into which an aggregate is divided for the purposes of sampling, each unit being regarded as indivisible when the selection is made. The definition of unit may be made on some natural basis such as households or persons, or upon some arbitrary basis such as areas defined by grid coordinates on a map.

selection with probability proportional to size. A sampling procedure in which the probability of a unit being selected is proportional to the size of the unit.

self-weighting sample. A sample in which the raising factors of the sample units are all equal. A self-weighting sample, usually in relation to the total population, is generally incorporated into a sample design to simplify tabulation work, because the population total is easily estimated from the sample total.

sex ratio. The number of males per hundred females, at birth, in a whole population, or in particular age groups of a population.

singulate mean age at marriage (SMAM). A measure of mean age at first marriage, derived from a set of proportions of men or women who are still single at different ages, and not derived directly from records of the ages of brides and bridegrooms.

stable population. A population with an unchanging rate of growth and an unchanging age composition, because age-specific birth and death rates have remained constant and there has been no migration over a long period of time.

stunting. The failure of an organism to attain full natural height, due to long-term nutritional inadequacy or disease. In the Nepal Nutrition Status Survey it is defined as less than 90 percent of the height-for-age reference median from the U.S. National Academy of Sciences.

total fertility rate (TFR). The average number of children who would be born alive to a woman during her lifetime if she were to live through all her childbearing years and conform to all the age-specific fertility rates of a given year.

truncation bias. A systematic distortion in rates calculated from collected data, due to the lack of some of the information needed to calculate the rates.

urbanization. Increase in the proportion of urban population to the total (rural and urban) population.

vital rates. Measures of the frequency of births, deaths, marriages, and divorces in a population.

vital registration system. A government-run system that attempts to record all of the births, deaths, marriages, and divorces in a population as they occur.

wasting. The sudden loss of weight due to acute starvation, malnutrition, or disease. In the Nepal Nutrition Status Survey it is defined as a weight-for-height ratio less than 80 percent of the reference median from the U.S. National Academy of Sciences.

REFERENCES

Acharya, B.N.

1976   Interdependence of cottage industry and the ecological situation. In *Mountain Environment and Development,* pp. 71—84. Kathmandu: Tribhuvan University Press.

American Public Health Association

1979   *A Health and Population Brief, Kingdom of Nepal.* (Mimeographed.) Washington, D.C.: American Public Health Association, International Health Programs.

Arriaga, Eduardo E.

1968   *New Life Tables for Latin American Populations in the Nineteenth and Twentieth Centuries.* Population Monograph Series, No. 3. Berkeley: University of California.

Barclay, George W., Ansley J. Coale, Michael A. Stoto, and T. James Trussell

1976   A reassessment of the demography of traditional rural China. *Population Index* 42(4):606—35.

Beyer, John

1975   The economic parameters of a population policy in Nepal. In *Workshop-Conference on Population, Family Planning and Development in Nepal,* pp. 80—102. Berkeley: Nepal—University of California Family Planning/Maternal and Child Health Project.

Blaikie, P.M., J. Cameron, D.J.P. Feldman, A. Fournier, and J.D. Seddon

1976   *The Effects of Roads in West Central Nepal.* 3 vols. Norwich: Overseas Development Group, University of East Anglia.

Bogue, Donald J., and Louise Rehling

1974   *Techniques for Making Population Projections.* Family Planning Research and Evaluation Manual No. 12. Chicago: University of Chicago, Community and Family Study Center.

Bourini, A.K.

1976   *The Demographic Sample Survey of Nepal, 1974—1975.* Kathmandu: Central Bureau of Statistics.

1977   *The Demographic Sample Survey of Nepal, Second Year Survey, 1976.* Kathmandu: Central Bureau of Statistics.

Campbell, J. Gabriel, Ramesh Shrestha, and Linda Stone

1979   *The Use and Misuse of Social Science Research in Nepal.* Kathmandu: Tribhuvan University, Research Centre for Nepal and Asian Studies.

Chauhan, R.S.

    1971   *The Political Development in Nepal 1950–1970.* New Delhi: Associated Publishing House.

Chhetri, N.B., B.N. Dahal, P. Egger, and G.B. Tamang

    1976   The voice of the farmer. In *Mountain Environment and Development,* pp. 157–63. Kathmandu: Tribhuvan University Press.

Chidambaram, V.C., John G. Cleland, and Vijay Verma

    1980   Some issues of survey methodology and data quality: the WFS experience. Paper presented at the annual meeting of the Population Association of America, Denver.

Coale, Ansley J.

    1971   Age patterns of marriage. *Population Studies* 25(2):193–214.

Coale, Ansley J., and Paul Demeny

    1966   *Regional Model Life Tables and Stable Populations.* Princeton: Princeton University Press.

David, A.S.

    1969   Nepal: national development, population, and family planning. *Studies in Family Planning* 1(42):6–16.

Dhital, B.P.

    1975   Population growth and agriculture. In D.C. Upadhyaya and Jose V. Abueva, eds., *Population and Development in Nepal,* pp. 97–114. Kathmandu: Tribhuvan University Press.

Eckholm, Erik P.

    1976   *Losing Ground: Environmental Stress and World Food Prospects.* New York: W.W. Norton.

Energy Research and Development Group (ERDG)

    1976   *Nepal: The Energy Sector.* Kathmandu: Tribhuvan University, Institute of Science.

Feeney, Griffith

    1979   A technique for correcting age distributions for heaping on multiples of five. *Asian and Pacific Census Forum* 5(3):12–14.

Frisch, Rose E.

    1978   Population, food intake, and fertility. *Science* 199:22–30.

Fuller, Gary, Robert Gardner, and Kanthi Ratnayake

1980   Areal fertility in Sri Lanka. Paper presented at the annual meeting of
the Association of American Geographers, Louisville, Kentucky.

Gaige, Frederick H.

1975   *Regionalism and National Unity in Nepal.* Berkeley: University of
California Press.

Goldman, Noreen, Ansley J. Coale, and Maxine Weinstein

1979   *The Quality of Data in the Nepal Fertility Survey.* Scientific Reports
No. 6. London: World Fertility Survey.

Gubhaju, Bhakta B.

1974   *An Abridged Life Table Construction for Nepal for the Period 1961–
1970.* (Mimeographed.) Kathmandu: Nepal Family Planning/Ma-
ternal and Child Health Project, Research Planning and Evaluation
Division.

Gurung, Harkha

1969   *Regional Development Planning for Nepal.* Kathmandu: His Majesty's
Government, National Planning Commission Secretariat.

Hagen, Toni

1961   *Nepal: The Kingdom in the Himalayas.* Bern: Kümmerly Frey,
Geographischer Verlag.

Hajnal, John

1953   Age at marriage and proportions marrying. *Population Studies*
7(2):111–36.

International Bank for Reconstruction and Development (IBRD)

1974   *Nepal Agricultural Sector Survey,* Vol. 3. Washington, D.C.

India, Department of Agriculture

1967   *Soil and Water Conservation in Nepal: Report of the Joint Indo-Nepal
Team.* New Delhi: Government of India.

India, Office of the Registrar General

1971   *Census of India 1971, Series 1–India, Special Monograph No. 1,
Birth Place Migration in India, Section III. Population Classified by
Place of Birth.* New Delhi.

Joshi, Bhuvan L., and Leo E. Rose

1966   *Democratic Innovations in Nepal: A Case Study of Political Accultur-
ation.* Berkeley: University of California Press.

Karan, Pradyumna P., in collaboration with William M. Jenkins

1960   *Nepal: A Cultural and Physical Geography.* Lexington, Kentucky:
          University of Kentucky Press.

Kramer, Roger G.

1979   *Nepal.* Country Demographic Profiles Series. Washington, D.C.:
          U.S. Bureau of the Census.

Krotki, Karol J., and Harsha N. Thakur

1971   Estimates of population size and growth from the 1952–1954 and
          1961 censuses of the Kingdom of Nepal. *Population Studies* 25(1):
          89–103.

Kumar, Satish

1967   *Rana Polity in Nepal.* New York: Asia Publishing House.

Myers, Robert J.

1940   Errors and bias in the reporting of ages in census data. *Transactions
          of the Actuarial Society of America* 41 (Part 2):411–15.

National Academy of Sciences, Committee on Population and Demography

1979   *Demographic Estimation: A Manual on Indirect Techniques.*
          (Mimeographed.) Washington, D.C.

Nepal, Central Bureau of Statistics (CBS)

1967   *Results of the 1961 National Census,* Vols. 1, 2, and 3. Kathmandu:
          His Majesty's Government, National Planning Commission Secre-
          tariat, Central Bureau of Statistics. (In Nepali.)

1975a   *Population Census–1971,* Vols. 1, 2, and 4. Kathmandu: His
          Majesty's Government, National Planning Commission Secretariat,
          Central Bureau of Statistics.

1975b   *Population Census 1971: Abstracts.* Kathmandu: His Majesty's
          Government, National Planning Commission, Central Bureau of
          Statistics.

1977   *The Analysis of the Population Statistics of Nepal.* Kathmandu:
          His Majesty's Government, National Planning Commission Secre-
          tariat, Central Bureau of Statistics.

1978   *The Demographic Sample Survey of Nepal, Third Year Survey,
          1977–1978.* Kathmandu: His Majesty's Government, National
          Planning Commission Secretariat, Central Bureau of Statistics.

1979   *Mid-term Population Sample Survey 1976 (National Level Result).*
          Kathmandu: His Majesty's Government, National Planning Com-
          mission Secretariat, Central Bureau of Statistics.

Nepal, Centre for Economic Development and Administration (CEDA)

1973   *Migration in Nepal: Implications for Spatial Development.*
         Kathmandu: CEDA, Tribhuvan University.

1977   *Migration in Nepal: A Study of Far Western Development Region.*
         Kathmandu: CEDA, Tribhuvan University.

Nepal, Department of Statistics

1958   *Census of Population, Nepal 1952/54 A.D.* Kathmandu: Depart-
         ment of Statistics (presently known as Central Bureau of Statistics).

Nepal, Family Planning/Maternal and Child Health Project (FP/MCH Project)

1977   *Nepal Fertility Survey, 1976. First Report.* World Fertility Survey
         Nepal Project. Kathmandu: His Majesty's Government, Ministry of
         Health, Nepal FP/MCH Project.

Nepal, Institute of Medicine

1975   *Rural Health Needs: Report of a Study in the Primary Health Care
         Unit (District) of Tanahu, Nepal.* Kathmandu: Tribhuvan Univer-
         sity, Institute of Medicine, Health Manpower Development Research
         Project.

Nepal, Ministry of Food, Agriculture and Irrigation

1977   *Agricultural Statistics of Nepal, 1977.* Kathmandu: His Majesty's
         Government, Ministry of Food, Agriculture and Irrigation.

Nepal, National Planning Commission

1975   *Fifth Plan (1975–1980).* Kathmandu: His Majesty's Government,
         National Planning Commission. (In Nepali.)

Nepal, National Planning Commission Secretariat

1974a   *Population Policy of Nepal: Report of the Task Force.* Kathmandu:
         His Majesty's Government, National Planning Commission.

1974b   *Draft Proposals of Task Force on Land Use and Erosion Control.*
         Kathmandu: His Majesty's Government, National Planning Com-
         mission.

1978   *A Survey of Employment, Income Distribution and Consumption
         Patterns in Nepal, Summary Report* (Vol. 4). Kathmandu: His
         Majesty's Government, National Planning Commission Secretariat.

Nepal, Population Policies Coordination Board

1976   *Conference on the Implementation of Population Policies.* Jointly
         sponsored by Nepal Population Policies Coordination Board,
         Nepal Ministry of Health, and Nepal–University of California FP/
         MCH Project. Kathmandu.

New York Times
1977   Rain and shortages aggravate resurgence of malaria in India.
            September 5, p. 3.

Okada, Ferdinand E.
1970   *Preliminary Report on Regional Development Areas in Nepal.*
            Kathmandu: His Majesty's Government, National Planning Com-
            mission.

Panday, K.K.
1976   The livestock, fodder situation, and the potential of additional
            fodder resources. In *Mountain Environment and Development,*
            pp. 47–60. Kathmandu: Tribhuvan University Press.

Pande, Badri Raj
1975   A review of family planning and MCH programme in Nepal. In
            *Workshop-Conference on Population, Family Planning and De-
            velopment in Nepal,* pp. 141–51. Berkeley: Nepal–University of
            California Family Planning/Maternal and Child Health Project.

Population Council
1967   Declaration of population. *Studies in Family Planning* 16:1.

Rana, Ratna S.J.B.
1971   *An Economic Study of the Area Around the Alignment of the
            Dhangadi-Dandheldhura Road, Nepal.* CEDA Study Series, No. 1.
            Kathmandu: Centre for Economic Development and Administra-
            tion.

Rana, Ratna S.J.B., and Yadav S. Thapa
1975   Population migration: nature and scope. In D.C. Upadhyaya and
            Jose V. Abueva, eds., *Population and Development in Nepal,* pp.
            43–77. Kathmandu: Tribhuvan University Press.

Ratnayake, Kanthi, and Gary Fuller
1980   An analytic atlas of Sri Lankan fertility. Unpublished manuscript,
            East-West Population Institute, Honolulu.

Regmi, Mahesh C.
1971   *A Study in Nepali Economic History, 1768–1846.* New Delhi:
            Manjusri Publishing House.

1978   *Thatched Huts and Stucco Palaces: Peasants and Landlords in
            19th-Century Nepal.* New Delhi: Vikas Publishing House.